Doogan

Other books written or edited by Mike Doogan:

Fashion Means Your Fur Hat is Dead:
A Guide to Good Manners and
Social Survival in Alaska

How to Speak Alaskan

Our Alaska:
Personal Stories from the Far North

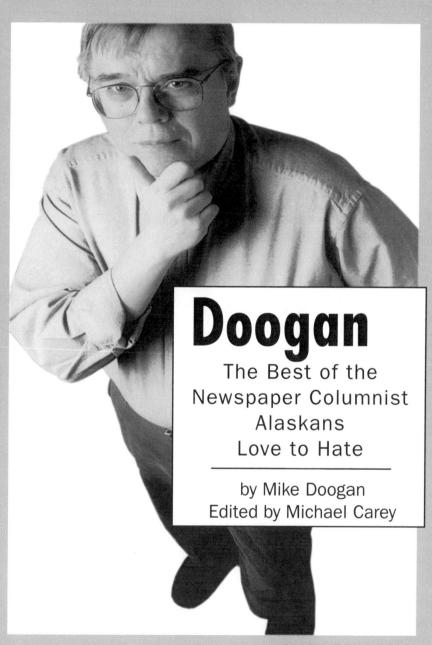

Doogan

The Best of the Newspaper Columnist Alaskans Love to Hate

by Mike Doogan
Edited by Michael Carey

EPICENTER PRESS
Alaska Book Adventures

Epicenter Press is a regional press founded in Alaska whose interests include but are not limited to the arts, history, environment, and diverse cultures and lifestyles of the Pacific Northwest and high latitudes. We seek both the traditional and innovative in publishing nonfiction books, and contemporary art and photography gift books.

Publisher: Kent Sturgis
Aquisition Editor: Lael Morgan
Cover and Book Design: Victoria Sturgis
Proofreader: Sherrill Carlson
Printer: Haagen Printing
Bindery: Lincoln & Allen Co.

Library of Congress Control Number: 2003112518

ISBN 0-9724944-5-6

Booksellers: This title is available from major wholesalers. Retail discounts are available from our trade distributor, Graphic Arts Center Publishing Co., PO Box 10306, Portland, OR 97210. Phone 800-452-3032.

PRINTED IN THE UNITED STATES OF AMERICA

First Printing

10 9 8 7 6 5 4 3 2 1

To order single copies of DOOGAN, mail $14.95 plus $4.95 for shipping (WA residents add $1.30 state sales tax) to: Epicenter Press, PO Box 82368, Kenmore, WA 98028.

Discover exciting ALASKA BOOK ADVENTURES! Visit our online Alaska bookstore at www.EpicenterPress.com, or call our 24-hour, toll-free hotline at 800-950-6663. Visit our online gallery for Alaskan artist Jon Van Zyle at www.JonVanZyle.com.

ACKNOWLEDGMENTS

Sometimes I feel sorry for newspaper columnists who don't get to write about Alaska. They don't have the vast and glorious physical canvass for a backdrop. Nor do they have the wonderful, awful cast of characters parading in front of it. My only regret about spending so much of my career chronicling Alaska is that my writing often fails to do justice to the people and events I have seen and heard.

No book is ever the work of one person. In that regard, I want to especially thank the newspaper's librarian, Sharon Palmisano, for her assistance in assembling this material.

As for the material itself, whatever isn't up to snuff on these pages is my sole responsibility, while what may be of merit is due mainly to two men and one women. The men are Howard Weaver, who offered me a column and stuck with me even when he must have regretted it, and Pat Dougherty, who has been and continues to be a perspicacious editor. The woman is, of course, my wife, Kathy, who is a valuable sounding board, a trusted critic, and sometimes, the center of a column as she is my life.

CONTENTS

Foreword, *13*

Preface, *15*

1   After More than 40 Years, Couple Plans Return to
Town They Loved, *18*

2   Ah, To Be Young Again and Reading Up on Adverse
Possession, *20*

3   Andrews-Mee Leaves 'Em Laughing, and Grateful,
After 35 Years, *23*

4   As You Get Older, Jump-starting the Day Gets More
Complicated, *26*

5   At the Heritage Center, the Big Draw is Person-to-Person
Contact, *29*

6   Behind the Wheel is not the Proper Place to Read Your Mail, *32*

7   Big Family Crowds Little Church to Watch a
Favorite Member Wed, *34*

8   The Century, Not the Millenium, Was Important For Alaska, *37*

9   Christmas Day Brings Back the Memories of
Many Big Meals, *40*

10   Cold House Evokes Memories from the
Waning of the Coal Age, *42*

11   Coming Home to This Primitive Outpost Ain't
What it Used to Be, *45*

12 Deadly Collision Prematurely Ends a Bicyclist's Simple, Happy Life, *48*

13 Despite Alzheimer's, Vera Gazaway Still Knows Her Own Mind, *51*

14 Dividend Isn't Perfect, But So Far No One Has Offered Better Idea, *54*

15 Double Vision Interferes With Attempts to Treat Children as Adults, *57*

16 Even The Low-Brow Can Find Culture in, of All Places, Fairbanks, *60*

17 Ex-Firefighter Punished for a Crime that Prosecutors Couldn't Prove, *63*

18 Face Plant Proves Gravity Isn't Our Friend, *66*

19 For Bubba-John, Fund-Raising Season Is No Time to Celebrate, *69*

20 Forget the Anchovies, How About Some King Salmon with That Pizza?, *72*

21 Girl Scout Cookie-Pusher Gang Putting Anchorage on the Edge, *75*

22 Graduation is the Chance for Parents to Bask in Reflected Glory, *78*

23 Holidays are a Little Less Happy Thanks to Bad Christmas Music, *81*

24 Iditarod's Anchorage 'Start' is Where Myth and Marketing Meet, *84*

25 If a Miner Must Be an Optimist, Then Roger Burggraf
Qualifies, *87*

26 If the Election's an Auction, Why Not Spare Voters?, *90*

27 If I Drove an Oscar Mayer Wiener, Everybody
Would Be in Love With Me, *93*

28 If It's Good Enough for the Kennedys, Why Not Try
Auction Here?, *96*

29 If You Liked 'Dances With Wolves, 'You'll Love Talks
With Animals,' *99*

30 Juneau Woman Works to Heal 'Raw, Open Wound'
of DWI Tragedy, *102*

31 Knowles Embarrasses Alaska to Advance His Political Career, *105*

32 The Last Trip to the Vet's is a Difficult and
Melancholy Journey, *108*

33 Law says a Bird is Not an Animal, So Marie Can Keep
on Honking, *110*

34 Legal System Provides Scant Justice in Little
Boy's Beating Death, *113*

35 The Lives of Our Mothers are More Than Taking
Care of Children, *116*

36 Look! In the Sky! It's a Bird! It's a Plane! No, It's (Still) Dadman!, *118*

37 Malone Put the Good of Alaska, and Open
Public Process, First, *121*

38   Maybe What Makes an Alaskan is as Simple as
Loving Alaska,   *123*

39   Naming Dead is Something Bagoy 'Always Felt Had
To Be Done',   *126*

40   Nenana Ice Classic is Alaska's Way to Pay Court to Lady Luck,   *129*

41   New Alaska Code Doesn't Seem to Include
Stopping to Help,   *132*

42   Nome Likes Richard Foster Machine Guns, Silencers,
Mortar and All,   *135*

43   Non-Thinkers Spotted Satan at Work in the
Homer Post Office,   *138*

44   Nothing Says "Be My Valentine" Better Than a Flamethower,   *141*

45   A Real Alaskan's Time to Get Ready For Winter
is After it Arrives,   *144*

46   Sadly, Some People Just Seem to Let the Darkness
Get to Them,   *147*

47   Saving Animals is a Full-Time Job Requiring
High-Protein Intake,   *150*

48   Shakespeare Was Wrong; Our Real Salad DaysArrive
with Age,   *153*

49   Shocking Tabloid Claim: 120-Year Old Eskimo
Woman Predicts Future,   *156*

50   The Smallest Rituals Are a Comfort to Those Dealing
with Death,   *159*

51 Sometimes it's Too Easy to Forget How Much Alaska
Means to Us, *161*

52 Tomatoes Not Only Cheap Crop That Could Be
Growing in Fairbanks, *163*

53 Usually People Cause the Problems, But It's the Bears
That Die, *166*

54 "Victim 5: 'I Want That Felony Assault to Stick to
His Record'", *169*

55 Wealth of Show Biz Experience Helps Harper Cope
with Adversity, *172*

56 When a Daughter Goes Off to College, a Father Begins
to Feel Old, *174*

57 Whoa, Dude, on Television This Alaska Place is,
Like, Totally Funny, *176*

58 With the Help of Database and $16 Dress,
Wedding is a Success, *179*

59 Woman Gets $2,600 Worth of Good News From Post Office, *182*

60 You Have to Grow Old, But Here's Proof You
Don't Have to Grow Up, *185*

About the Author, *189*

FOREWORD

Gene Roberts Legendary editor of the *Philadelphia Inquirer*, admonished writers to "make the readers see." Col. Robert McCormick, fiery *Chicago Tribune* publisher, instructed his reporters to "comfort the afflicted and afflict the comfortable."

Mike Doogan, Metro columnist for the *Anchorage Daily News*, is all that and more. Doogan is read from Kotzebue to Ketchikan and sometimes what he makes his readers see isn't pretty. And his hell-raising is not always appreciated within the establishment's inner circles.

More than one GOP stalwart has told me "I never read Doogan," as if shunning him was a matter of honor. But that didn't stop a Republican who never reads Doogan from adding, " I recently was in the doctor's office where my eyes were drawn to a Doogan column on a chair. I couldn't help reading it, and he made me so mad . . ."

Some would say Doogan is a born contrarian. He certainly is contrary to the rich, powerful, and pretentious. Yet, often enough, Doogan also lets readers see themselves gently reflected in columns about his family, home, neighborhood, and memories of childhood growing up in Fairbanks. When Doogan writes that his garage bulges with so much junk and bric-a-brac "that it looks like the lost-and-found at U-Haul," he speaks for many Alaskans.

Doogan is equally inclined to write about the dog pound, the bus system, snow-clogged streets, and the every-day guy who has an exceptional experience or faces an unusual problem. Mike has mastered the art of the brief portrait, the short profile of Alaskans who have made the state a better place—or just made it damned interested.

Mike Doogan's Alaska is a place where people find themselves—and lose themselves. Where dreams are born—and shattered. Where newcomers wonder if they have been around long enough to become "real Alaskans"—and sourdoughs complain that they have seen the last of the Last Frontier.

Doogan's Alaska also is home to a changing cast of opinionated characters who will be heard on all subjects. Mike is, so to speak, their interpreter.

An old editor once told me "all a writer has to offer is his experience, and he must reveal his experience to the readers." Mike Doogan knew that instinctively. His fellow Alaskans have been richer for it.

Michael Carey, editorial page editor,
Anchorage Daily News, 1990-2000

PREFACE

Early in 1990, I was working as an assistant city editor for the *Anchorage Daily News* when the newspaper went in short order from having two local columnists to having none.

The people who ran the newspaper needed to fill that hole PDQ. My entire job interview went like this.

Howard Weaver, the newspaper's top editor at the time, called me into his office and said, "Would you like to be our Metro columnist?"

"Yes," I said.

"You are," he said.

Being right down the hall wasn't my only qualification for the job. I'd lived in Alaska all my life and, for most of my adult years, had worked as a journalist. Being an Alaskan meant I knew it all, and being a journalist gave me the tools to find out the trifling little details.

Still, I didn't know anything about writing a newspaper column week in and week out, so I cast around for advice. The novelist Pete Dexter, who was working at the time as a columnist for the *Sacramento Bee* gave me two pieces of advice I've never forgotten.

"Don't try to be somebody you're not," he wrote to me. "If you are in the paper regularly, you won't be able to fool people about who you are."

And, he said, don't tense up. Just give them the best story you've got that day.

The other thing I read that has stayed with me is something *San Francisco Chronicle* columnist Stephanie Salter once wrote, which went something like this: My job is not to give a weighty analysis of anything, my job is to write down what I see and say, Whoa, creepy.

I've been following these three pieces of advice for going on 14 years now. I have written more than 1,500 columns and more than 1 million words.

I write three kinds of columns. Some are about my life, and the lives of people close to me. Some are about interesting people doing interesting things. Some are about the state's politicians and their shenanigans.

I try to get people to think, which isn't easy. Most people have their opinions and prejudices firmly set and readily available in handy slogan form. If I can't get people to think, I try to inform them. If I can't inform them, I try to entertain them. If I can do one of these, I'm satisfied. If I can do all three, I'm amazed.

This approach isn't exactly a ticket to popularity. I've been picketed and threatened, reviled on talk radio and in letters to the editor. Doesn't bother me. This is Alaska, after all. And, to paraphrase Brendan Behan, wherever there are two Alaskans there are three opinions.

Besides, I've been at this long enough to have won a grudging acceptance in most quarters. Not everyone likes what I write, but these days the response is more like what one fellow once told a friend of mine: I don't agree with a word he writes, but at least the son of a bitch says what he thinks.

ONE

AFTER MORE THAN 40 YEARS, COUPLE PLANS RETURN TO TOWN THEY LOVED

For four years, from 1951 to 1955, the Johnsons lived in a raw little frontier town called Anchorage. Charles is 80 now, Helen 79...

Helen Johnson and her husband, Charles, have lived their entire lives in Cincinnati, Ohio. Almost. Their house is only about a mile from the spot where Charles was born. Helen's parents moved there when she was a year old. They grew up there, went to school there, met and married there, had children there, watched the kids grow up and leave home there, retired there. You'd have to dig down a good long ways in that fertile Ohio soil to find the place where their roots begin.

But that almost has been nagging at them, particularly Helen, for more than 40 years now. This year, she's doing something about it. For four years, from 1951 to 1955, the Johnsons lived in a raw little frontier town called Anchorage. Charles is 80 now, Helen 79, but in August they plan to return for the first time, with as many children and grandchildren as they can muster, to, as Helen put it in a letter she sent to the editor here, "renew our love affair with Alaska."

It's a wonderful letter, full of the homey details of a young family with growing children. Charles came here to work for the Army Corps of Engineers, bringing his wife, 6-year-old Scott and 4-year-old Janet. Their third child, Todd, was born here.

Janet won the Shrine Circus coloring contest when she was 8. She's an architect now in Vancouver, B.C. Scott went on to serve in the military, then to a career in city government — he was city manager of Cincinnati for a while — before going to Romania with USAID. He was always a serious fellow, like the time, well, let Helen tell it.

"In 1953 our son Scott applied to the *Anchorage Times* for a newsboy's job at a nearby shopping center," she wrote. "After his first day on the job he returned home. A neighbor boy came to call for him and when asked what he was doing, in his 8-year-old, self-assured voice he replied, 'I am with the *Anchorage Times.*'"

I recognized that story when I read it. My mother has a few like that about me, and your mother has some about you, too. Scott is 52 now, but I'll bet that every time he hears that story he's 8 again.

When Charles left the Corps, he went to work for local architect Ed Crittenden. The Johnsons bought a lot off Fireweed Lane, then the edge of town, and were planning to put a pre-fab log house on it. But during breakup the mud was so thick it almost sucked their boots right off, so they put their house up on 15th instead.

The Johnsons might have settled here permanently. But Helen's father died, leaving her mother alone. And Charles' parents wanted their only son near them. In the end, the call of family was stronger than the call of the frontier, and they returned to Cincinnati.

"It was the right thing to come back," Helen said.

Even after all these years, Helen's fondness for the bygone Anchorage reached right through the telephone when I talked with her. She recalled the sunrises over the Chugach, the good times at the First Presbyterian Church, "the dearest place in our hearts," being able to get out and paint watercolors of Anchorage scenes.

She said she understands that Anchorage is a lot bigger now, a lot different. But that doesn't make any difference. When I asked why she was coming back after all these years, she didn't hesitate.

"We're coming back to love it," she said. "We loved it then."

MARCH 30, 1997

Two

AH, TO BE YOUNG AGAIN AND READING UP ON ADVERSE POSSESSION

*All this sounds interesting enough in its own way. But I never had
any urge to study the law, and I found I wasn't getting a big
kick out of studying it by proxy either.*

Our daughter went back to law school today. She arrived at
the airport three weeks ago with two suitcases and a bulging
backpack.

"Here, Dad, you take this one," she said.

I could barely lift the bag off the floor. It took us a long time
to get to the car because I had to stop for rest every 20 feet.

"What's in this thing?" I huffed as I horsed it into the back of
the car. "Bowling balls?"

"Books," she said. "I have to study."

At her school, Christmas break isn't Christmas break. It's a
reading period, with tests when she gets back.

"That doesn't seem fair," I said when I first heard about the
schedule. "They had the same sort of deal my freshman year in
college. Ruined Christmas for me. Nothing like yuletide joy mixed
with fear and loathing."

"It's not so bad," my daughter said. "These electric lights they've
invented since you were in school make studying much easier."

Having our daughter at home is like having three people visit.
It doesn't take more than a day or two for every flat surface to
be covered with her stuff. Whenever the phone rings — and it

rings a lot — it's for her. And her ideal place to study is in the middle of the living room, where everyone else can study along with her.

"Ah, it's the Van Valkenburghs and the Lutzes," she announced with glee, looking up from an 8-pound law book. "This is an important case on adverse possession."

Learning the law, it turns out, is something like learning auto mechanics or some other trade. In order to learn how to handle a particular legal matter, you study how others have handled it in the past. So you read cases. Like auto mechanics, though, the law is always being changed by a better, or craftier, way of doing things. Just when you've learned the legal version of how to fix a carburetor, some wise guy goes to court and invents the legal version of fuel injection.

All this sounds interesting enough in its own way. But I never had any urge to study the law, and I found I wasn't getting a big kick out of studying it by proxy either.

So I replied, "Don't you think the Van Valkenburghs and the Lutzes would be more comfortable down in your room?"

Part of the problem, maybe all of it, is that I'm envious. At first I thought I was just envious of the freedom I recall from my own college days. No mortgage payments. No bosses. No daily deadlines. But then I realized I was envious in another way too.

When your children are young, they look to you as the source of all knowledge. In fact, as they get older, they drive you batty with "how comes" and "because whys." For a long time, even after they are in school, you are their sage and their encyclopedia.

In most cases, that lasts until they get to subjects you don't remember well or never knew. Then they decide that since you don't know everything, you don't know anything. This is a phenomenon widely known as the teen years. If you all live through that, a child might consult you on some things. But all too often that child takes a track that leads her into what is, for you, un-known territory.

This visit has made it clear to me that our daughter is on such a track, a track that is likely to be exciting and challenging and fun. I'm happy for her, but I'm envious too. She gets to go exploring while I stay home. I suppose it's not really her learning the law I'm envious of. It's her being young.

JAN. 7, 2000

THREE

ANDREWS-MEE LEAVES 'EM LAUGHING, AND GRATEFUL, AFTER 35 YEARS

"When somebody tells me, 'I voted for Ted,' I say, 'That's great, but we represent everybody,'" she said.

You have to say this for Barbara Andrews-Mee: She's no quitter. She's worked for the same fellow for 35 years.

"I have been with Ted Stevens longer than I have been with three husbands," she said last week with a characteristic laugh. "It's been a great ride."

The ride ends this month, when Andrews-Mee retires as manager of U.S. Sen. Ted Stevens' Anchorage office.

Resplendent in a red plaid blazer, Andrews-Mee sat in Stevens' big office in the federal building and talked about her time with Alaska's senator-for-life. Her own office, next door, was stacked with files she's trying to clean out. Her desk, which once belonged to Stevens' predecessor, Bob Bartlett, was a jumble of of notes and letters. Propped atop a filing cabinet was a big, black-and-white photo of a younger Stevens, looking like his dog had just died, with a hand-lettered caption that read: Whoever said it would be easy?

Maybe it hasn't all been easy, but for Andrews-Mee it seems to have been fun. The woman is a pistol. Here's just a sample:

On her height (she's 5-feet tall): "I tell people I used to be 6-foot-2, and then I went to work for Stevens."

On her age (she's 59): "Jeez, that's hell, when you have to admit your kid's going to turn 40."

On why she never ran for office herself: "Oh, no, my skin is too thin. Like the fellow who goes to a football game and when they go into a huddle, he thinks they're talking about him."

On the fancy new computer she has at home: "We've got the whole thing. Don't get off at Chicago if you're going to New York."

On her plans for retirement: "My god, I am my mother. You know how you just become your parents? My mother was a holy terror ... 89 when she died and still dyeing her hair red ... I'm not going to sit home and watch soaps."

Instead, she said, she's going to play golf — she's still trying to break 100 — serve on the Defense Advisory Commission on Women in the Services, and do volunteer work.

"It's payback time," she said. "my country and my state and my community."

Andrews-Mee went to work for Stevens when he was just another lawyer with political ambitions. He was first elected to the state Legislature in 1962, before there was the oil money to pay legislative staff.

"In those days, Ted would find somebody going to Anchorage and give them three, four Dictaphone belts, and I'd type them up and send them back," she said. "And that's how we did legislative mail."

Stevens' political success since then owes a lot to Andrews-Mee. His office has a long-standing reputation for solving constituents' problems, whether or not the constituent is a Stevens supporter.

"When somebody tells me, 'I voted for Ted,' I say, 'That's great, but we represent everybody,'" she said.

That attitude is a big part of the reason so many Democrats enter the voting booth every six years and quietly cast a ballot for the Republican. One way and another, Andrews-Mee has made her boss a lot of friends.

So it seems appropriate, out of respect for the job she's done, to let Andrews-Mee say she's been happy to do that for Stevens, to let her sneak in one last plug for her boss.

"He's done a great job," she said. "Why else would I stay with somebody for 35 years."

MAY 18, 1997

FOUR

AS YOU GET OLDER, JUMP-STARTING THE DAY GETS MORE COMPLICATED

The last of the hot water is gone, and I can't remember any more of the words to "The Mighty Quinn." So I get out of the shower.

When I was a boy, I could leap out of bed and into the day in minutes. Not anymore. Here is the process I go through to get on my way to work.

7 a.m. My alarm goes off. I push the snooze button and go back to sleep.

7:10 a.m. My alarm goes off again. I push the snooze button and go back to sleep again.

7:20 a.m. My alarm goes off again. I turn my alarm off and go back to sleep.

8 a.m. The woman who lets me live with her wakes me up and tells me I am going to be late. Then she gets into the shower.

8:10 a.m. I stumble out of bed, put on my robe and slippers and grope my way to the bathroom. The woman who lets me live with her wishes me a pleasant good morning. I remind her of what happened to Janet Leigh in similar circumstances. I brush my teeth. For the thousandth time I wonder why no one makes a coffee-flavored toothpaste. I drag myself to the kitchen, pour coffee, go into the living room and sit in a chair. Sometimes a classical music CD is playing. Sometimes I stop to put one on. If the shades are open, I stare into my back yard. If they are not, I stare at the shades.

8:20 a.m. I take my first sip of coffee. I make my first decision of the day. I will not go back to bed.

8:30 a.m. The woman who lets me live with her comes boiling out of the bedroom ready to take on the world. She collects her things, all the while talking to me cheerfully. Before I can strangle her, she leaves. I go back to staring and drinking coffee.

8:40 a.m. I finish my first cup of coffee. Time for the second decision of the day: Should I have another cup of coffee, get into the shower, or eat breakfast? If I'm going to have to make these decisions all day, I think, maybe I will just go back to bed. I opt for more coffee.

9 a.m. No more putting off the shower.

9:15 a.m. The last of the hot water is gone, and I can't remember any more of the words to "The Mighty Quinn." So I get out of the shower. Shave. Go look at my wardrobe. The choice of pants is easy; most of mine still won't fit from my holiday eating binge. A shirt is harder, particularly since I have been told more than once it should "go with" the pants. Go where with the pants? I asked. That got me nothing. I pick something I'm pretty sure won't cause outright laughter at work. Get dressed.

9:30 a.m. I sit at the kitchen table with my third cup of coffee and a bowl of cereal. I get out my calendar and a pad and plan my day. I love planning my day. It's like planning to do something is an accomplishment all by itself. I make a list of the things I'm going to do that day. When I'm finished, I decide that felt so good that I'll plan the next day, too. Sometimes I get so giddy I plan a whole week.

9:50 a.m. I throw things into my backpack. Get something together for lunch. Then I hunt for the Lost Thing. Some days the Lost Thing is the badge I need to get into the building at work. Some days it is my watch. Some days it is my checkbook. Mostly I find the Lost Thing, but some days it stays lost. I always hope that doesn't mean there will be two Lost Things the next day.

10 a.m. I go out the door and start my car. Sometimes I have to sweep it and scrape it. I am backing out of the driveway when I remember the Forgotten Thing. So I have to drive back up the driveway, turn off the car and go back into the house. The Forgotten Thing is usually some papers, or a book I promised to bring someone or my briefcase for school. The nice thing about the Forgotten Thing is that it is almost always easier to find than the Lost Thing.

10:10 a.m. I get back into the car and get going. A couple of blocks from home, I remember the Other Forgotten Thing. Mostly, I just keep driving. I really should have been at work by 10 a.m.

MARCH 28, 1998

FIVE

AT THE HERITAGE CENTER, THE BIG DRAW IS PERSON-TO-PERSON CONTACT

What did this summer's visitors like best?
"The people," Nelson said. "They liked the interaction,
they liked being able to meet Alaska Natives."

Poldine Carlo, a lively, smartly dressed Athabaskan lady of 78, sat on the stage at the Alaska Native Heritage Center on Saturday, telling stories about her life. Her audience was about 50 people when she began but swelled as others were drawn in ones and twos by her musical voice.

Carlo talked of many things: the village where she was born, Nulato, the arranged marriages of her grandparents' time, leisurely boat trips to the neighboring village of Koyukuk. But mostly she talked about change.

"I have seen a lot of change in my lifetime, from the time I start remembering until now," she said.

The heritage center is both a monument to that change and a bulwark against the cultural deterioration it has caused. As a modern Alaska tourism enterprise, it drew about 70,000 visitors in its first season, according to Margaret Nelson, the chief operating officer. But "the center is not just an attraction for visitors," said Nelson, a Tlingit from Juneau. "Our mission is to be a gathering place that celebrates, perpetuates and shares Alaska Native culture."

The center is nestled in the birch and cottonwood off Muldoon Road, near the Glenn Highway. It consists of a main building, called the Welcome House, and a series of structures around a small lake that display the lifestyles of Alaska's main Native groups: a pole-roofed log cabin for the Athabaskans, a Yupik men's house, an Inupiat winter house, a long house of the Aleut and, still under construction, a Tlingit clan house. Everyone suspects that local visitation has been held down by the admission price, $19.95. On Saturday, the center dropped its price to $5 for a community appreciation day, and several hundred well-bundled-up people showed up to look it over.

In addition to storytellers like Carlo, the center offers visitors Native dance groups and Native artists at work, photo displays of Native lifestyles, and glass cases full of their handicrafts and artwork. There's a theater with a video of Native life, a gift shop, a snack bar and the outdoor displays, each with an attendant to answer visitors' questions. What did this summer's visitors like best?

"The people," Nelson said. "They liked the interaction, they liked being able to meet Alaska Natives."

Demaris Hudson is one of the people they met. She's a bubbly 19-year-old Athabaskan from Tyonek who spent the summer as an attendant at the log cabin.

"Oh, it's been just great talking to people," Hudson said, "and I lost my voice like 10 times this summer just talking. And it gave me a chance to learn some of my language, some of the words like 'house' and 'smokehouse' from my grandfather." She met people from all over the world, and learned more about the cultures of other Native groups.

"Like when the Tsimshian dancers were here, I'd never seen their dances before," she said. "I learned their songs just listening, and on their last day, it was my day off, I was just standing and watching and singing."

The combination of information and personal contact seemed to go down well with Saturday's crowd, particularly once Greg Nothstine, the Inupiaq World Eskimo and Indian Olympics athlete, brought out his hide blanket and gathered a group of tourists and performers to toss people into the air.

Anthea Dare, a 27-year-old visitor from Adelaide, South Australia, pronounced her blanket-assisted flight "great." She and her companion, 24-year-old Sydneysider Phil Wulff, said the heritage center has a lot to offer.

"We've been looking for something like this that shows the lives of the Indians, what their lives are like, all through Canada and Alaska," Wulff said. "And this center is perfect."

SEPT. 26, 1999

Six

BEHIND THE WHEEL IS NOT THE PROPER PLACE TO READ YOUR MAIL

They turn the driving experience from a communal effort to get us all where we are going as safely and quickly as possible into a free-for-all.

A scene from the streets of Anchorage.

I'm headed north on Lake Otis and stop at the light at 36th. The woman in the turn lane to my left is reading her mail. The woman behind me is talking on her cellphone. The woman in the lane to my right seems to be searching for something in her back seat. Two cars, both driven by men, pull into the intersection and stop, prevented from turning left onto Lake Otis by oncoming traffic.

The light changes. Both cars turn through, even though the light facing them is now red. They have plenty of time, though, because the woman in the turn lane, who now has a green arrow, is still reading her mail. Someone honks. The woman waves angrily, as if she is irritated at being disturbed, and drives off. Others follow. Two cars, both driven by men, turn through after the arrow turns red.

The light in front of me is now green. I pull away. In my rearview mirror, I can see the woman behind me still sitting there, talking on her cellphone. The other lane of traffic isn't moving, either, because the woman who was looking for something still has her head buried in the back seat. I can only imagine what the drivers behind them are muttering, if they aren't too busy changing CDs, reading the paper or putting more sugar in their lattes to notice.

Anchorage is an often dangerous place to drive. In 1999, the most recent year for which there are complete statistics, 10,700 accidents were reported to the Anchorage Police Department. That's a five-year high: more than one accident an hour, 24 hours a day, every day. People were killed in 19 accidents, and were injured in almost 2,500.

The dark, the snow, the icy streets all make driving here difficult. Far more dangerous are the drunks, speeders and red-light runners, all too often guys in battleship-sized pickup trucks, who we have to share the streets with. In part, they drive this way because they are confident they can get away with it.

I'm not sure how many traffic laws I saw broken at that stoplight. But I did see lots of examples of another sort of behavior, people treating driving as a part-time occupation. This behavior may be adding to the danger on the streets by increasing the frustration of other drivers with scant self-control. It certainly adds to my sense that Anchorage contains more than its fair share of careless, selfish drivers.

When somebody drives down the street talking on a cellphone, it's a statement: My time is more valuable than your safety. When a woman reads her mail instead of watching the light, she's making a slightly different statement: My time is more important than yours. What these actions have in common, with each other and with those of drunken drivers, speeders and red-light runners, is that they put the desires of individuals above the safety and convenience of the group. They turn the driving experience from a communal effort to get us all where we are going as safely and quickly as possible into a free-for-all.

There's no excuse for this. Keep your eyes and your mind on the road. Leave your telephone calls and mail for later. And if you're such a big shot you can't, hire a chauffeur.

FEB. 16, 2001

BIG FAMILY CROWDS LITTLE CHURCH TO WATCH A FAVORITE MEMBER WED

We also discussed the events since the last big family gathering, and sorted out who was feuding with whom at the moment.

I spent the weekend awash in family. My own family of four drove up the Parks Highway from Anchorage, and dissolved instantly into the larger family like a raindrop falling into a pond. I never did get a precise count of uncles, aunts, nieces, nephews, first cousins, first cousins once removed, husbands, wives and what not, but a painstaking analysis of the bushels of photos taken would put the number somewhere between 50 and 100. The oldest was nearly 80; the youngest, 3 months.

We were gathered for the wedding of my niece, my older brother's oldest daughter. She is immensely popular with the rest of the family, which accounts for the turnout, and is the first of her generation to marry. The wedding took place in the Catholic church by the Chena River, technically the Immaculate Conception Church, but called by everyone in town The Little Church. What with the bride's family, friends, family friends, and a substantial contingent of the groom's family here from the East Coast, there was some concern the church would prove too little. It wasn't, barely.

The Little Church was built in 1904, and moved across the frozen river to its current location in 1910. It is being renovated this summer, so the guests walked past piles of dirt trucked in for landscaping and up brand-new wooden steps to get into the church. The temperature outdoors was in the 70s; inside, it was a good 20 degrees warmer. People were soon fanning themselves with copies of the wedding program.

When you return to the place you grew up, the oddest things trigger sharp memories. The summers are warm here; temperatures in the 80s aren't unusual and the fanning reminded me of all the summer Sundays in church, with people trying to stir the hot, still air with their parish bulletins. The Mass was similar to the one of my youth, but different enough to remind me that I wouldn't be out playing baseball as soon as I shed my good clothes.

After the wedding, the crowd moved across the river to the Eagles Hall. There, without the constraints of formality, we spent a lot of time figuring out which of the seldom-seen kids belonged to which of the cousins. Hard enough, since we all look somewhat alike. Even harder, because the family seems to have settled on a small number of mainly Irish first names. Turns out the groom's family did, too, and so did the big, Irish families in attendance. Anyone who'd shouted "Kathleen" would have been answered by about 10 percent of the women and girls present. So we are forced to use a family shorthand.

"This is Kitty Ed's youngest," one of my cousins said, offering me a gurgling baby.

We also discussed the events since the last big family gathering, and sorted out who was feuding with whom at the moment. Being part of a big family has many rewards, but tranquility isn't one of them.

We hear a lot about family values these days. Mostly, that phrase is used by the religious right to mean anti-abortion, anti-gay, anti-science, anti-intellectual. But the values my family has taught me are inclusive, not exclusive. Tolerance is one. Blood might be thicker than water, but it doesn't wash away the irritations of many strong personalities at close quarters. Humility is another. It's tough to be snooty with people who remember all your childhood disasters. Patience and open-handedness, a sense of duty and self-control are valuable, too.

None of these things makes us the Brady Bunch. But they do help make us a family.

JUNE 12, 1994

EIGHT

THE CENTURY, NOT THE MILLENNIUM, WAS IMPORTANT FOR ALASKA

In 1900, the brand-new Gold Rush town of Nome was Alaska's biggest city, numbering about 12,000. Skagway, the second-largest city, had 2,012 residents, while No. 3 Juneau had 1,456.

One thing that has been lost in the glitter of the end of the millennium is the end of the century. In a city that is 85 years old and a state that is 40, the century was far more important. When 1000 rolled around, life in Alaska continued pretty much as it had 1,000 years before that and 1,000 years before that. But between 1900 and 2000, Alaska really changed.

"The total population of Alaska, as shown by the returns of the Twelfth Census, is 63,592," according to the report of the 1900 census. Of those people, nearly half — 29,536 — were Alaska Natives, 145 were other native Alaskans, and the rest were immigrants.

Most immigrants had arrived during the previous three years, brought north by the Klondike Gold Rush. They were overwhelmingly white; the enumerators counted just 168 Negroes, 269 Japanese and 3,116 Chinese.

According to the most recent estimates, those for 1998, Alaska's population has increased about tenfold, to 621,400. The number of Alaska Natives has more than tripled, to 103,287, but their share of the population has dropped to about 20 percent. Whites number 459,463 and are a huge majority, 74 percent of the total population. The percentage of African Americans, who number 27,652, is up slightly, while the percentage of Asians and Pacific Islanders, who number 30,200, is about the same. Hispanics, who were not counted in the 1900 census, were estimated in 1998 at 28,889.

Alaska Natives were fairly evenly split between men and women in 1900, but the immigrants were overwhelmingly men. Among whites, 30,948 were men and 3,200 were women. Among the Chinese, 3,113 were men and three were women. For women, the odds were very, very good. But the goods were no doubt very, very odd.

Today, Alaska Natives remain evenly split between men and women, and women have closed the gap overall to about 48 percent of the population. There still are more men than women in every ethnic group but not many more.

In 1900, the brand-new Gold Rush town of Nome was Alaska's biggest city, numbering about 12,000. Skagway, the second-largest city, had 2,012 residents, while No. 3 Juneau had 1,456. Neither today's biggest city, Anchorage at 258,782, nor its second-largest, Fairbanks with 83,928, existed then. Today, Nome and the surrounding area have 9,402 residents. Eight hundred and fourteen people live in the city of Skagway, while Juneau numbers 30,236 residents.

The differences between the population of today and that of 100 years ago stretch across the board. My favorite statistic is that in 1900, government work accounted for 1.9 percent of Juneau's total employment. But in broad terms, the major changes are these: Alaska's population is bigger, whiter, more female and more urban.

Other changes aren't so easy to quantify. But here are some things to think about. In 1900, the primary mode of transportation in Alaska was walking, followed by boating when the ice allowed. The main tools were the ax, the pick and the shovel. The fastest form of communication was the letter. The main form of lighting was the kerosene lamp, and the primary kitchen appliance was the wood stove. The main occupation categories were "hunters, guides, trappers and scouts," followed by "miners and quarrymen." Just over 1 percent of the population worked in offices.

Then there were the changes occurring throughout the nation. Here's just one: In 1900, a typical man could expect to die at age 46; a typical woman, 48. By 1997, life expectancy reached 74 years for men and 79 for women.

If Alaska changes as much in the next century as it did in the one ending tonight, it will be a very different place indeed.

Dec. 31, 1999

NINE

CHRISTMAS DAY BRINGS BACK THE MEMORIES OF MANY BIG MEALS

Twenty-five pounds of solidly frozen turkey takes a while to thaw. The usual technique was to put it into cold water...

One way and another, I managed to spend half of my Christmas Days with my feet under my parents' table. When I lived with them and, later, when I lived in the same town as they did, Christmas dinner was a command performance. My father did both the commanding and the performing.

I don't recall my father cooking very often. My mother, then my sisters, did the day-to-day cooking. But until age caught up with him, my father always cooked on Christmas. His food was never very exotic, but there was a lot of it.

Here is a typical Christmas menu: turkey, stuffing, mashed potatoes, gravy, sweet potatoes with marshmallows, fruit salad, green salad, a green vegetable, cranberry sauce, olives, rolls, and pumpkin pie and apple pie, both with whipped cream. Nothing much but milk or water to wash it down with — growing up in Alaska had not made my father a wine connoisseur — and coffee with dessert.

Just thinking about these meals gives me a stomachache.

When I was a kid, there were only two kinds of food available in a Fairbanks grocery store: canned and frozen. That meant a frozen turkey, and, believe me, in Fairbanks in December that bird was unconditionally frozen. Since a family dinner was never a small affair, the turkey was usually upwards of 25 pounds.

Twenty-five pounds of solidly frozen turkey takes a while to thaw. The usual technique was to put it into cold water — I know that doesn't make sense, but it worked — for a few days, then stick it into the refrigerator until the big day.

I'd like to tell you what happened next, but I don't know. My father was happy to leave the initial preparations to whomever could be dragooned into making them. But that laissez-faire attitude vanished when it came time to cook. No one was allowed in the kitchen. So we had to content ourselves with trying to figure out where everyone was going to sit — there were never enough chairs — and listening to the crash and clatter of pots and pans and, occasionally, to colorful language.

Sometimes my father would call out for something and someone would be dispatched to the store. I think the last run I made was for pimientos. Otherwise, we rarely saw or spoke to the cook. That created a certain difficulty, because dinner was always late. I suppose trying to get everything on the table hot was a challenge, but waiting was an equal challenge. Things could get tense. After some of us had our own children, we always sent the smallest, cutest child into the kitchen to ask about dinner.

Once dinner was on the table, we ate. My father made sure of that. He considered it a personal insult if someone left the table without waddling. It was considered only good manners to have thirds.

I eat much more sensible holiday meals now that my parents are gone. The day has none of the tension, either. Still, I'd give a lot to have one more Christmas dinner with my mom and dad.

But at least I have my memories. I hope you have yours, too. And that, if you are lucky this Christmas Day, you are making some more.

DEC. 25, 1901

TEN

COLD HOUSE EVOKES MEMORIES FROM THE WANING OF THE COAL AGE

And on those rare occasions when, for mysterious reasons, the fire went out, who do you think they blamed? Me. Can you believe it?

I woke up last week in a cold house.

"The pilot light on the furnace is out," the woman who lets me live with her said. "I'm calling the plumbing and heating guy."

"Wait a minute," I said, "why not let me see if I can fix it?"

"We can't afford a new furnace right now," she said. "We're still paying off those kitchen repairs."

I couldn't quite see my breath inside the house, but the temperature certainly speeded up my morning routine. I don't believe I've ever gone from the shower to fully dressed faster. Of course, I ended up wearing different-colored socks, and I later discovered I had my underwear on backward, but there's really no time for fine-tuning at 37 degrees. I was out the door and on my way to work before my towel hit the floor.

I did even less work than usual that day. I just wasn't prepared. My morning routine involves a lot of lollygagging, and I missed it. What's the use of dawdling over a cup of coffee if you have to break the ice to get a drink?

All in all, the morning reminded me of my youth. I grew up in a big, old, drafty house in Fairbanks that had started out as a small cabin and grown in do-it-yourself fits and starts. From the moment we moved into it, the house was difficult to heat. The furnace was designed for a much smaller place. The only insulation was old newspapers and pieces of cardboard box. And after the dog started leaving the back door open — my older brother taught it to open the door but not to close it — things really cooled off.

This had its advantages, though — even in winter. You could leave food out of the tiny refrigerator without having it go bad. You could tell how cold it was outdoors by measuring the frost that crept under the front door. And a kid didn't have to take many baths. The bathroom was in a particularly rickety addition, and running a tubful of hot water caused such a dense fog that adults couldn't tell who was in the tub. I once went for six glorious months without a bath, simply by claiming that one of the compulsive weekly bathers was really me.

But the advantages pretty much evaporated when my older brother handed down to me the job of keeping the furnace going. The basement made the black hole of Calcutta look like a suite at the Ritz, and I had to descend into it daily to fill the stoker with coal and clean out the firebox. And on those rare occasions when, for mysterious reasons, the fire went out, who do you think they blamed? Me. Can you believe it?

This experience left me scarred in many ways, not the least of which is that I didn't receive the training to deal with a gas furnace. I'm from the Coal Age; it would be like asking a Neanderthal to play Nintendo.

The truth is, I did once have a chance to learn about gas heat. It finally got so cold that my father installed a propane space heater in the kitchen. My job, he told me, was to get up very early in the morning, go downstairs and light the heater.

But you know what? It was darn cold before the heater was started. So I taught my younger brother to do the job. I got away with that for months, but when my father finally figured out what was going on, he blew up.

"Are you out of your mind?" he roared. "He's only 7."

"So?" I said. "This job isn't hard. Crack the valve. Light a match. Piece of cake."

"If he does it wrong," my father bellowed, "he'll blow this place to kingdom come."

I looked at my dad for a long time.

"OK, I can see your point," I said at last, "but why is that a problem?"

I hope whatever the plumbing and heating guy did to my furnace fixed the problem. I don't really need any more reminders of that conversation with my father. Or what happened next.

APRIL 25, 2000

ELEVEN

COMING HOME TO THIS PRIMITIVE OUTPOST AIN'T WHAT IT USED TO BE

I've been coming and going from Alaska my whole life, and from Anchorage for the past 32 years. I've been happy to go, and even happier to come back.

As I was jouncing my way home from the airport last week, along narrow, icy, rutted streets lined with dirty snow, I thought to myself: Primitive outpost. I live in a primitive outpost.

People in the rest of Alaska like to talk about Anchorage like this is Seattle's northernmost suburb. I suppose if you're just off the airplane from McGrath, the half-dozen tall buildings and countless strip malls might make Anchorage seem downright urban. But if you are flying in from California, this looks much more like a part of the frontier than a part of modern America.

Particularly right now. The town's a mess. The city government seems to be hauling less snow and spreading more dirt on the roads, making Anchorage both grungy and inconvenient. The mayor might want this to be the city of lights and flowers, but right now, when the lights are out and the flowers aren't blooming, what we've got is the city of narrow streets and mudpies.

I've been coming and going from Alaska my whole life, and from Anchorage for the past 32 years. I've been happy to go, and even happier to come back. But that gap is narrowing, and I'm not sure why.

True, there are many aspects of California life that are appealing. As I sat poolside, drinking coffee and reading the morning paper, I thought to myself: I could get used to this. The lawns and shrubs were green, the flowers were blooming, and the birds were singing in a hundred-part chorus. There was, in abundance, everything Anchorage lacks most of the year.

A gentle climate is only part of the appeal. Museums, theaters, baseball parks, bookstores; you name it, they've got more, bigger, better, richer. I'd wager that there are more different kinds of restaurants in a six-block stretch of San Francisco's Clement Street than in all of Anchorage. And if you don't like any of them, just grab a cab to another street. If you don't like the restaurants in Anchorage, you're in for a long airplane flight.

But that's always been true. Just as we have more man-made stuff than McGrath, California has more man-made stuff than we do. That is offset only in part by the fact that it has more bad man-made stuff, too. The air is often foul, the water tastes of chemicals. There is an aggressive panhandler on every street corner in every downtown in every city. Driving is an enterprise that takes up more time the farther south you go. I suppose crime is worse, too, but the closest I got to a crime was being asked to pay $1.67 for a small bag of peanuts in the San Francisco airport.

And when it comes to stuff man doesn't make, California is not in the same league as we are. There's nothing like the mountains we see every day, or the salmon that the more skillful of us catch from time to time. As my editor said when I told him of my impression, "If you're a trout fisherman, a primitive outpost is the place to be."

So it's a trade-off, balancing the good and bad of living here against the good and bad of living somewhere else. For me, the balance is still clearly in favor of here, just not so much.

Why not? Maybe it's like a friend of mine says, that Alaska winters accumulate like mercury poisoning. One day you just can't do it anymore. Maybe it's early childhood training. When I was growing up, people retired to warmer climes, where they sat in front of their trailers with other Alaskans and talked about Alaska. Maybe it's that the state has changed. What was once a society of people, however quarrelsome, moving forward together has become a collection of whining me-firsters.

Or maybe it's just that when a rube goes to the city, he comes home dazzled.

MARCH 12, 1996

DEADLY COLLISION PREMATURELY ENDS A BICYCLIST'S SIMPLE, HAPPY LIFE

At the funeral, several people said Patrick wasn't really in the casket, but in their hearts and minds. He might not have had much, but he had friends.

A couple of dozen people turned up on a snowy Saturday morning to say so long to Patrick Humpal. The ceremony at Kehl's mortuary on the Old Seward Highway was simple. Patrick's brother, Paul, said a few words. His mom, Geraldine, talked about Patrick and read from Scripture. Friends got up to say goodbye. Some cried.

Patrick was killed on Gambell Street last week. He was riding his bicycle like always, when he got hit by a cab. You might have seen his crumpled bike lying in the street on TV, or read the story in the newspaper. It was just a few lines. Patrick wasn't famous.

"He was just an everyday guy leading an everyday life," Paul said.

Patrick was a few days shy of his 39th birthday when he died. He was born in Saginaw, Mich., his mom said, and graduated from high school in Marquette. He did all kinds of work with his hands, but he was best at electrical. He lived in Georgia for a while, then California, before he came here in 1988.

"He really loved living up here," Paul said.

Patrick did electrical work for contractors, and for people who heard about him by word of mouth. He also worked off and on at the Post Office Mall, fixing things, painting, shoveling snow.

"He tried to help people all the time," said William Hamilton, who owns the coin shop in the mall on Fourth Avenue.

Patrick knew enough about electrical work to get a journeyman's card, but he never passed the test. He took it once but didn't do well. Hamilton said he figured maybe Patrick just wasn't good at tests. But Paul said it was something else.

"He did not want to be a boss. He wanted to work," Paul said. "'He figured if he got his journeyman's card, they'd make him a boss."

A simpler life seemed to suit Patrick. He didn't live on the street, exactly, but close to it. He slept in a tent as much of the year as weather would allow. When winter set in, he found a place to fix up for room and board, or a trailer someplace.

"I just emptied his storage locker," Paul said, "and my mom and I were saying to each other, 'Here's a 38-year-old man and everything he owns is in a 3-by-3-by-3 box.'"

But Patrick seemed happy, doing what he liked.

"He liked to ride bicycles and party," said Grady LeBlanc, who knew Patrick from Bean's Cafe.

"He was the most unbelievable bike rider I've ever seen," said Larry Casey, who works in one of the state offices in the mall. "He used to stop at my house in Eagle River, drink a six pack with me, strap another to the back of his bike and ride to Wasilla."

Riding his bike made Patrick a top fund-raiser the past couple of years for the American Lung Association of Alaska. He rode in the Clean Air Challenge, a two-day trip from Anchorage to Talkeetna, bringing in about $500 each year in $1 and $2 and $3 pledges. He got in the habit of dropping by the lung association office.

"We were always happy to see him," Jo Lamson said. "Now that this has happened it's kind of like a kick in the stomach. We should have found out more about him and we should have known him better."

At the funeral, several people said Patrick wasn't really in the casket, but in their hearts and minds. He might not have had much, but he had friends. And it was clear that he'd lived and died doing what he wanted to do.

"He was real happy with who he was and what he was doing," Paul said. Which is, when you think about it, about the best epitaph a man could have.

Nov. 23, 1997

THIRTEEN

DESPITE ALZHEIMER'S, VERA GAZAWAY STILL KNOWS HER OWN MIND

Helping to remove that stigma is one of the reasons that Vera agreed to be the spokeswoman for the Alzheimer's Association's annual memory walk tomorrow.

Vera Gazaway always knew her own mind.

As a young woman during World War II, she wanted to join the new Women's Army Corps. Her husband, Prentiss, who was fighting in Europe, was against the idea. Vera joined up anyway. That, she says, brought so many irate letters from her husband that it caused talk in her unit.

"But eventually he forgave me," she said.

Vera knew her own mind in going back to college after the war to get a master's degree and in becoming a teacher. She and Prentiss moved around quite a bit before settling in Alaska in 1953. They lived in Palmer and then Juneau, having kids and raising them. After Vera retired, they moved to Anchorage.

Vera knew her own mind well enough to know that a life of retired leisure wasn't for her. She became the director of the Older Person's Action Group and editor of the Senior Voice, starting or helping out on many programs for senior citizens.

But Vera doesn't know her own mind so easily these days. Two years ago, she was diagnosed with Alzheimer's disease.

Alzheimer's is a form of dementia, a group of diseases that lead to the loss of mental and physical functions. Its cause is unknown.

The official estimates are that 4 million Americans have Alzheimer's, about 4,000 of them in Alaska. The chances of getting the disease increase with age. According to Liz Hunt, who works for the Alzheimer's Association Alaska Chapter, about 10 percent of 65-year-olds have Alzheimer's, about 15 percent of 75-year-olds, about 50 percent of 85-year-olds.

"Early onset Alzheimer's can affect people in their 30s, 40s and 50s," Hunt said. "But most of the victims are seniors."

Vera is 77. She reacted to her diagnosis with characteristic practicality. She moved into the Pioneers Home, which specializes in the care of people with dementia, and began to study the course of her own disease in the hopes she might learn something that would help others.

"I started a diary when I was diagnosed and I have been very faithful," she said.

Her diary has grown to a row of notebooks that are arranged neatly above the small, white desk in the small, white room where Vera lives. They contain copies of test results and doctors' notes and her own handwritten observations.

"I'm finding out that some days I know where I am and some days I don't," she said.

She's also no good at all with numbers anymore, she said, and sometimes not so good with names or dates. When I asked her when her family settled in Alaska, she said, "Gosh, we moved around so many times and Alzie's not helping me at all."

A person can live 20 years or more after being diagnosed with Alzheimer's, but the average span from diagnosis to death is six to eight years. Because of that, and because the disease makes its victims less and less lucid and more and more helpless, Alzheimer's has something of the same stigma cancer once had, particularly among the old.

Vera got a taste of that when she moved into the Pioneers Home.

"Somebody said, 'What brings you here' and I said, 'I've got Alzheimer's.' Silence."

Helping to remove that stigma is one of the reasons that Vera agreed to be the spokeswoman for the Alzheimer's Association's annual memory walk tomorrow. The walk is part fund-raiser, part memorial to people killed by the disease and part consciousness-raising effort. It begins at 10 a.m. at the University of Alaska Anchorage sports center.

But it is clear that another reason Vera is telling her story is that she is just not going to give in to Alzheimer's.

"I can either sit around and say, 'Woe is me,'" she said, "or I can do something interesting."

So, for now, it seems Vera Gazaway still knows her own mind.

Sept. 15, 2000

DIVIDEND ISN'T PERFECT, BUT SO FAR NO ONE HAS OFFERED BETTER IDEA

People who want to change the dividend program talk about endowing their pet project or pumping the money into state government. These are worse ideas than the dividend.

I'm having second thoughts about the Alaska Permanent Fund dividend.

Maybe it's the size of the check. The dividend burst through the $1,500 barrier for the first time this year. The increase from the previous year, $243, is the largest in the dividend's history. This is starting to seem like real money.

Maybe it's how gleefully the media trumpets the announcement. There's a week of guessing and other hype leading up to the revelation of the amount, which is streamed across the bottom of TV shows and trumpeted in front-page headlines. I suppose it has to be this way; the amount of the dividend is big news. But it's all a little unseemly.

Maybe it's how vigorously businesses vie for the money. The checks will start hitting bank accounts in two weeks, and their arrival will cause a big bump in consumer spending. Practically everybody who sells anything will have a dividend deal going: car dealers, airlines, furniture stores, you name it. This is only smart business, I guess, but it is accompanied by more than a whiff of greed.

I don't have any second thoughts about the Permanent Fund itself. Saving some of the oil money, at a time when there was far too much to spend wisely, was a smart move. I don't have second thoughts about how the fund is managed, either. The only other option was a development bank, and if we'd done that the money would be gone by now. Ask anybody in Alberta, where they frittered their money away on "province building."

But the dividend? I don't know about the dividend. I've taken every one of them — $14,776 worth, give or take. A guy like me, who works for a paycheck, can't afford the nobility of just sending the dividend back. To tell the truth, I'm not sure I'd have the nobility even if I didn't have 101 uses for the money. Still, I have to wonder what the dividend is doing to Alaska.

Some people don't like the dividend because they say it will make Alaskans expect something for nothing. I don't agree. Alaskans already expect something for nothing. They don't pay any state taxes, yet they expect all sorts of state goods and services. "Something for nothing" could be the state motto.

Other people say the dividend will make Alaskans selfish. I don't agree. Alaskans are already selfish. That's why our elections have become promising contests, won by those with the simplest slogans and the narrowest views of the world. "No new taxes!" "Hands off the Permanent Fund!" "English only!" "No compromise on subsistence!" People don't come here for the climate or culture. They come here to get theirs or because they think they can do things here that aren't possible in more civilized areas. They come here to please themselves.

Does the dividend encourage this kind of thinking? You bet. It encourages hypocrisy, too. The same people and politicians who complain the loudest about welfare are the first to rush to the defense of the dividend. The only difference is that people on welfare have to show they need the money.

But what's the alternative? We could do something selfless with the money — help find a cure for cancer, try to help out the Russian Far East, put it into the space program — but we haven't got the vision or leadership for anything like that. People who want to change the dividend program talk about endowing their pet project or pumping the money into state government. These are worse ideas than the dividend.

That's where my second thoughts have taken me so far. Alaska is a place of extremely limited political options at the moment. The dividend may not be a perfect program, but it's better than anything else we are likely to do.

Lucky for us, huh?

SEPT. 25, 1998

FIFTEEN

DOUBLE VISION INTERFERES WITH ATTEMPTS TO TREAT CHILDREN AS ADULTS

I understand that some parents get around these difficulties by becoming their children's friends. Then they can talk in a free-and-easy way about anything.

My daughter spent her summer herding little kids. Most days, she brought home tales of their escapades.

"We'd only gone half a block," she'd say of that day's field trip, "when the little girls started saying, 'I'm tired. Will you carry me?'"

These stories gave me double vision. With one eye I saw the young woman telling the story. With the other, I saw the little girl who came home from preschool complaining about a six-block walk to the park, saying, "I'm so tired. We walked all day."

My double vision gets me in trouble. She tells her story, I tell mine and, instantly, I am tried and convicted of failing to treat her as an adult.

"Oh, Dad," she says, rolling her eyes.

I'd appeal, but the fact is, I'm guilty. No matter how hard I try, I cannot treat my children as simply two more adults. Worse, I can't keep my mouth shut about it.

As a child myself, I know how irritating this can be. It's difficult to portray an adult convincingly when your mother is telling everyone about the time you shared a Popsicle with two cocker spaniels.

These sorts of stories are a way parents keep children in their place. I use them, too. There is no better response to one of my son's commentaries on the depravity of the human spirit than to ask him, "What would Mister Rogers say if he heard you talking like that?" As a boy, he couldn't get enough of calm, kindly Fred Rogers. The TV show was a high point of his day. He may have grown and matured since then, his view of the world may have darkened, but he has yet to develop a satisfactory response to that question. Particularly since he knows that behind it lies an arsenal of Mister Rogers anecdotes, each a reminder of who is the parent and who is the child.

If I could limit such comments to situations in which they are useful, all would be well. But I cannot. I am in danger of becoming that terror of families, a parent by reflex. Not quite the mother who sits next to her 40-year-old son at dinner, cutting up his meat, but certainly the sort of parent who sees many more situations requiring his counsel than his children do.

I'm having an especially tough time keeping my nose out of my daughter's decision about going to school abroad. I'm certain she's not old enough to live in a foreign country for six months, and I suspect she's not even old enough to pick which country she's not old enough to live in. How could she be? Just yesterday, I was giving her piggyback rides. So far, thank God, I have been able to avoid mentioning this in our conversations on the subject, but I feel myself weakening.

I understand that some parents get around these difficulties by becoming their children's friends. Then they can talk in a free-and-easy way about anything. I'd like to be one of those parents, but what about conflicts between the roles? My daughter is trying to decide between colleges in England and Australia. As her parent, I would tell her to go to England for the prestige. As her friend, I would tell her Australia will be more fun.

What I should do, no doubt, is keep my advice to myself, and agree with whatever choice she makes. But I've been her father all her life. So what I'll probably do instead is tell her that no matter how certain she is that she wants to go abroad, there was a time when she was just as certain she wanted to be a train driver.

That's OK. She's been my daughter her whole life, too. She won't be listening.

SEPT. 1, 1996

EVEN THE LOW-BROW CAN FIND CULTURE IN, OF ALL PLACES, FAIRBANKS

Now, let me say right here that I've got my own ideas about what's cultural and what ain't. Paintings should look like something—people and horses are good—and so should sculptures.

People in Fairbanks get mad if I hint their town might not be the most sophisticated place this side of Paris, France. When I was up there last week, for example, I got aired out one afternoon by a guy in fairly clean Carhartts, who said Fairbanksians are not louts. At least I think that's what he said. He had so much snoose between his cheek and gum it looked like he was sucking on a ground squirrel. Made him kind of hard to understand.

"You blanking linthead," he maybe said, "we've got blankety theater, we've got blankety toe dancing, we've got long-hair blankety music. We've got blankety-blank cul-tu-wer up the blankety-blank wazoo."

OK, so I made that up. Fairbanksians never wear fairly clean Carhartts in the afternoon. They're evening wear.

The part about ticking off the residents of the Golden Heart City, though, that's true. My own mother calls up to complain whenever I point out that Fairbanks' idea of nouvelle cuisine is Cajun curly fries. Or that the most-read book in the classics section of the city library is Mickey Spillane's *My Gun is Quick*. Or that when a Fairbanks resident refers to someone as "an artist," he's most likely talking about someone who has a particularly deft touch with diesel engines. Or a boning knife. Or someone who can chug an entire 16-ounce Pabst without spilling on his coveralls, then belch "The Alaska Flag Song."

OK, Mom, you can put down the phone. The truth is, Fairbanks does have culture. When I was up there a couple of weeks ago, I seen some.

Now, let me say right here that I've got my own ideas about what's cultural and what ain't. Paintings should look like something — people and horses are good — and so should sculptures. For performing arts, I prefer movies where people's heads explode. And if I get to see babe-errific actresses naked, so much the better. The movies have to be in English; if I want to look at something Italian, I order pizza. And when I want to settle down with one of the great books, I look for something with a corpse or a sea battle in it.

Believe it or not, some people consider this somewhat low-brow. I tell them, what did you expect? I was born and raised in Fairbanks. Art was the guy who ran the card game in the back room of the Sportland.

So I wasn't sitting in an auditorium in the University of Alaska Fairbanks' arts building because I needed a ballet fix. One of my nieces was going to dance. I was there more in tribute to the kid's toughness than anything else. She's danced through bone spurs and into tendonitis, and I figured if it was that important to her, I could sit still for an hour. Besides, her mother is my next-youngest sister, a woman who is not above punching me very hard on the shoulder.

The dancing was of several different sorts. I believe the novice dancers had one or two more collisions than were actually choreographed into their routine, but otherwise the audience seemed satisfied. I know I was impressed. Those kids did some things that made my hamstrings sore just watching.

I was equally impressed by what was going on around the dance performance. Every summer, several hundred kids from all over the state descend on the Fairbanks campus to do art of all sorts. On the final weekend, when I was there, kids were putting on plays, singing jazz and showing their prints, carvings and what have you. It was more culture than I'd seen in Fairbanks since I heard a guy play "Stairway to Heaven" on a flute made of variously full beer bottles.

Frankly, I was glad to see kids wallowing in art. Why, some day one of them might grow up to be a major cultural icon in Fairbanks. You know, first-class gold-pan painter. Soloist with the chain-saw orchestra. Moose-dropping sculptor. That sort of thing.

JULY 24, 1994

SEVENTEEN

EX-FIREFIGHTER PUNISHED FOR A CRIME THAT PROSECUTORS COULDN'T PROVE

Then he pronounced Roath's sentence like a man disappointed he didn't have more severe penalties, perhaps a term in the stocks, at his disposal: a $4,000 fine and 300 days in jail.

District Courtroom No. 4 has none of the grandeur of the post-Prudhoe palace of justice next door. With its no-nonsense cream-colored paint, hard wooden pews and stark fluorescent lighting, it is as plush and comfortable as a Puritan church. The courtroom is a place for disposing of the minor sins of modern life: simple assault, petit larceny, political incorrectness.

Friday, the confessed sinner was Gary Roath. The former Anchorage firefighter pleaded no contest to two counts of convincing young women he was a photographer for Playboy magazine, then taking pictures of them while they were naked.

The congregation was small: a few lawyers, a couple of cops, two women who'd posed, three reporters, a TV cameraman. Roath, a thin, ferrety-looking guy in a pin-stripe suit, sat quietly while people argued about just how grave his sins had been.

Grave indeed, said prosecutor James Fayette. Fayette is a short man with the face and attitude of one of Oliver Cromwell's Roundhead soldiers. He marched through the details of Roath's scheme: fliers announcing a Playboy contest, elaborate props at his temporary studio in a local hotel, release forms giving him ownership of the photos.

But, Fayette said, Roath's real motive in getting the women naked was "to allow sexual contact."

"The defendant touched them, touched them as he posed them, touched their genitals with glycerine," he said.

District Attorney Eddie McNally's office had treated Roath's escapade as a sex crime from the start, but didn't have the evidence to prove it. Instead, Fayette hit Roath with beaucoup commercial misdemeanors and a felony, the worst case of overcharging in this town since *Les Miserables* played the PAC. Friday, after he'd dropped most of the charges, he knocked those who'd questioned them.

"People that criticize this effort," he said, "in this prosecutor's opinion, are part of the problem."

He didn't say which problem. The general decline of moral standards? Men lying to women to get them to take their clothes off? Prosecutors not being able to charge defendants with whatever the heck they want?

Maybe the problem of topless dancers having their hopes dashed. When Roath asked them to pose, "a lot of our self-esteem and our pride came out," Jada Williams told the court. Like most of Roath's 10 models, Williams makes her living gyrating in public without clothes.

"A lot of us feel really stupid now," she said, "and a couple are camera-shy."

Roath's lawyer, Gentleman Jim Gilmore, tried to put the best possible face on his client's actions. Gilmore has a courtly air, enhanced by graying hair and half glasses. His description made the whole affair sound like an unfortunate business misunderstanding.

Anybody who'd spent even five minutes in a courtroom knew Gilmore was going to lose this battle. Throughout the lawyer's presentation, Judge Gregory Motyka squirmed and frowned like a man wrestling with the devil, breaking in more than once with hostile questions.

In a voice out of Brooklyn and a prosecutor's office, Motyka told Gilmore that the "days are long since gone" when Roath's malefactions could be considered just a business crime.

"The court has its suspicions of what Mr. Roath's ultimate (goal) might be," he said.

Then he pronounced Roath's sentence like a man disappointed he didn't have more severe penalties, perhaps a term in the stocks, at his disposal: a $4,000 fine and 300 days in jail. With time off for good behavior, that's $400 and 20 days for every woman photographed. Fayette couldn't charge Roath with a sex crime and Motyka couldn't convict him of one, but they did their best to punish him for one.

Hallelujah, brothers and sisters. Gary Roath got everything he deserved Friday. And then some.

SEPT. 21, 1993

EIGHTEEN

FACE PLANT PROVES GRAVITY ISN'T OUR FRIEND

I'm not complaining, mind you. Considering what has happened to some people in the past couple of weeks, and what may happen to others in the next couple, I got off easy.

I did a face plant on the Coastal Trail a week ago Friday.

Here's how it happened. I was doing a standard training run: A dozen or so miles, about 5:30 a mile. Nothing too strenuous for a superbly conditioned athlete like myself. I rounded a corner and saw an enraged moose attacking a group of children and nuns. I held the moose off with one arm and scooped kids and nuns out of the way with the other. As I grabbed the last little tyke from under the moose's hooves, the giant ungulate swerved and tripped me. With an armful of urchin, I had no choice but to land on my face.

The results weren't pretty . . .

OK, OK, that's not what really happened. And I didn't do it grabbing totally big air on in-line skates or swerving to avoid a black bear on a mountain bike. (But what a black bear was doing on a mountain bike, I'll never know.)

What really happened was that I was walking — briskly, mind you — when I stepped in a hole and turned my ankle. Some combination of physics and aging reflexes dictated that the first thing to hit the asphalt was my face.

(I figured I could tell any story I wanted because there weren't any eyewitnesses. I know that because as I walked back to my car, I didn't pass anyone paralyzed by laughter.)

Anyway, the results weren't pretty. The first result was that I bled all over a perfectly good Summer Solstice T-shirt. Not to mention the Coastal Trail and the inside of my car.

The second result was that I spent 5 1/2 hours in the emergency room. Why is it that everything happens so quickly in emergency rooms on television and so slowly in emergency rooms in real life?

After a few of those hours, a nurse walked past the room, stopped, and said, "Are you bleeding?"

I nodded.

"Do they know you're bleeding?"

I nodded again.

"OK," she said and walked on.

After X-rays and a CT scan and a couple of examinations and lots of bleeding, the verdict was: broken nose, pushed-in teeth, and fractured facial bones.

Believe me, among the phrases you don't want to hear from a doctor is "fractured facial bones."

"The bones over the sinuses here in the front of your face are very thin," he said. "It's kind of like an eggshell cracking."

It'll be awhile before I eat hard-boiled eggs again.

In the week since the trail assaulted me, I've been to a couple of doctor's appointments and a couple of dentist's appointments. The good news is that the bleeding stopped after 24 hours. The bad news is that anyplace my face is not scabbed over it is black and blue. Anyplace it is not either of those, it is yellow. I have a new bend in my nose and, for the first time at age 53, braces on my teeth. It's like having a mouth full of barbed wire.

Gravity, it turns out, is not our friend.

I'm not complaining, mind you. Considering what has happened to some people in the past couple of weeks, and what may happen to others in the next couple, I got off easy. But I won't be working for a few days. For one thing, it's tough to interview someone if they take one look at your face and run screaming from the room.

Soon, I'm told, I'll be as good looking as I ever was. Some goal that is. The swelling and bruising will go away and the doctor will reset my nose. The last time I saw him, he said he needed a good photograph to work from. I've looked around and couldn't find just the right thing. Maybe you can help. Do you have a sharp, full-face head-and-shoulders shot of Mel Gibson I could borrow?

SEPT. 30, 2001

FOR BUBBA-JOHN, FUND-RAISING SEASON IS NO TIME TO CELEBRATE

"You just don't know what it's like, Hoss," Bubba-John said. "Being a lobbyist at fund-raisin' time's like being a turkey at Thanksgiving."

This column is fiction. I mean, made right up. Any relationship between its contents and a real city named Anchorage, a real state named Alaska, or real politicians, whatever their names, is just damn fool luck.

The Whine Cellar was full of lobbyists. Some were holding their heads and moaning. Others were holding their stomaches and groaning. Bubba-John Derrick lifted a fizzing glass to his lips and winced.

"What's the trouble here, Bubba-John? Flu epidemic?" I asked as I sat down at his table.

"My check-writin' arm's plumb wore out," he said, setting the glass down. "I got me a headache too big to fit in my Stetson, and a case of heartburn that'd light up Lubbock. It's worse 'n flu season. It's legislative fund-raiser season."

The moaning and groaning increased at nearby tables when he said that. Suddenly, one of the lobbyists lurched to his feet.

"If I never see another one of them cocktail weenies, it'll be too soon," he cried.

"Tell it, brother!" someone shouted.

"The last fund-raiser I was at, the wine was so cheap the vintage was October," he yelled.

That brought shouts of "Amen!" and "You got that right!"

"I been to so many fund-raisers in the past two weeks," he called, "the entire Legislature thinks my initials are ATM."

He sat down to whistles and applause.

"Them oil company boys sure can testify," Bubba-John said.

"I don't see what you people are complaining about," I said. "When you're buying influence, you've got to pay sometime."

A tableful of women lobbyists began to softly sing "Nobody Knows the Trouble I've Seen."

"You just don't know what it's like, Hoss," Bubba-John said. "Being a lobbyist at fund-raisin' time's like being a turkey at Thanksgiving. Only they don't put you out of your misery. Everybody and his duck's havin' a party, and you got to show up at every one."

"Why not just mail in the check?" I asked.

Bubba-John gave me a pitying look.

"You gotta remember who you're dealin' with here," he said. "'Bout half of them legislators oughta be in Guiness for world's shortest attention span. You don't put the checks right in their hand, and you won't even be able to get in to see their staff during the session."

"Leads to some weird scenes, let me tell you," Bubba-John said. "Like that fund-raiser in the paper there, where the Republicans was standing behind Uncle Sam hats in separate rooms. I been to two goat ropings and a county fair, and I ain't seen nothing like that before. Except one time back in my youth, down Nogales way. But there it was one girl to a room and the back scratchin' was immediate.

"I tell you, it's rough. Two, three fund-raisers a night. Eatin', drinkin', signin' your name over and over again. Why, a couple of boys over to the Alliance skipped training camp and are out for the entire season. Tore their rotator cuffs tryin' to sign checks for the entire House majority at one sittin'.'"

"I expect, then, you all will be glad when the campaign financing reform initiative passes," I said. "You won't be able to give money."

"Your lips to God's ear, Hoss," Bubba-John said. "But that ain't what'll happen. It'll turn out each and every one of us has a grand-mother living in each and every election district. Or somethin'. Changin' the law is just changin' the loopholes."

He took another drink.

"But if it gets rid of these parties, I'm for it," he said. "And so's everybody else in the room. In fact, we're all just waitin' for those initiative people to hold a fund-raiser. I'm personally plannin' to give with both hands."

Nov, 14, 1995

TWENTY

FORGET THE ANCHOVIES, HOW ABOUT SOME KING SALMON WITH THAT PIZZA?

"I've seen a lot of people take a lot of fish out of Ship Creek," Roth said. "We guesstimate that we're between 750 and 1,000 kings harvested..."

I didn't see this myself, but a guy I work with swears he saw a pizza being delivered to the banks of Ship Creek one night a couple of weeks ago.

This is fishing?

"Actually, this is probably the only urban king salmon fishery in a city the size of Anchorage anywhere," local fish guy Kent Roth said. "And it is definitely unique, being in a heavily industrialized area like it is, to be able to have the opportunity to catch a 50- to 60-pound king salmon."

And if you want to plop that king on the barbie, it's better fishing than the Kenai River. None of this frou-frou catch-and-release stuff on Ship Creek. You hoist one of these bruisers ashore and it's yours, yours, yours.

Roth, who is actually the state Department of Fish and Game's assistant area management biologist, concedes that not every king in the creek weighs as much as a third-grader. But the department wants them caught, anyway. They are hatchery-built fish, and very few have any use beyond being grilled over mesquite chips.

"We're looking at between 2,500 and 2,750 total return," he said. "We'd like the anglers to harvest a good 80 percent of them."

People are turning out to oblige. The Ship Creek king fishery has been around for some time. I personally have been skunked there three years running but this is the first year that seven-day-a-week fishing has been allowed. So at weekend high tides, the joint is jumping.

"I've seen peak periods down there where we've had 600-plus people fishing in a single time," Roth said.

That's quite a crowd for the short stretch of creek in the railroad yards where fishing is legal. Monday afternoon, there were more like 60 than 600. It was just after dead low tide, and the creek was rushing through the deep channels, much of its muddy bottom exposed. No one was having much luck.

The fishing area has been spruced up this year. The Alaska Railroad abandoned the stretch of track that bridged the creek, eliminating one pedestrian hazard, and lined C Street with snow fence in an attempt to eliminate another. There are portable outhouses, and new, $1-a-car parking lots of the sort that cause outdoors columnists to whine. A roach coach makes the rounds at peak periods, and the ice cream man cruises the place. Even if you don't catch a fish, you don't have to go hungry.

And fish do get caught. Even during the lull Monday, a man was washing a freshly cleaned king that looked like it went 25, 30 pounds.

"I've seen a lot of people take a lot of fish out of Ship Creek," Roth said. "We guesstimate that we're between 750 and 1,000 kings harvested out of that stream already, which puts us well past last year."

If Roth gets his way, we're going to see more urban fishing.

"We're looking at Fish, Cottonwood and Wasilla creeks up in Knik Arm, and in the Anchorage area we're looking at Ship Creek, Campbell Creek and Bird Creek," he said. "All of these systems support some limited natural production. But none of them support enough for a sport fishery."

The plan, which still has to go through community councils, advisory committees and God knows what else, is to stock the other creeks with silver salmon. Ship Creek already gets them.

But Ship Creek's silvers aren't nearly as popular as the kings, which draw anglers at all levels of skill and experience. Why, I was washing a few lures a couple of weeks ago when a woman with two kids set up near me, and began to take their gear right out of the Pay 'n' Save wrappings.

"I think that's the unique opportunity of Ship Creek," Roth said, "It offers people that don't necessarily have the dollars or the time to travel to the Kenai Rivers or the Lake Creeks or the Deshkas, the opportunity to still catch one of the big fish."

Not to mention the opportunity to eat hot pizza while they're doing it.

June 21, 1991

Twenty-One

GIRL SCOUT COOKIE-PUSHER GANG PUTTING ANCHORAGE ON THE EDGE

I tell you, they are everywhere. It's a government conspiracy. I'll bet they even deliver the cookies to the pushers in black helicopters.

Anchorage is in serious trouble. No, I am not talking about the chance Tom Fink might be elected mayor. I am talking about a much more serious threat to civilization as we know it: Girl Scout cookies.

That's right, the annual tragedy is playing itself out all over town. The little pushers are everywhere, assaulting people in malls with high-pressure sales pitches like: "Would you like to buy some Girl Scout cookies?" Looking at their marks with big eyes. Smiling. Doing everything but saying, "Go ahead. Try them. The first one's free."

Why, they are so brazen that they come right up to the homes of respectable citizens in broad daylight to hawk their wares. The Scouts shove their cookie boxes right under the noses of upstanding members of the middle class in a blatant attempt to prey on their weaknesses for shortbread and lemon cremes and those really tangy strawberry ones.

What I want to know is: Where are the police when this is going on? It is obviously gang activity. These urchins wear gang colors — they call them uniforms, I'm sure — take a gang oath, have a gang motto. They even have younger groups of recruits, whom those in the know call "Brownies," who are being groomed for full membership in the gang. Children are getting kicked out of school every day for stuff much less blatant than this. Why don't the authorities crack down on this gang of cookie pushers?

I'll tell you why. Connections. Lots of important women have been Girl Scouts, and they are protecting current Scouts. Janet Reno used to be a Girl Scout. You can tell just by looking at her. Hillary Clinton has former Girl Scout written all over her. Donna Shalala? Girl Scout. Madeleine Albright? Total Girl Scout. I tell you, they are everywhere. It's a government conspiracy. I'll bet they even deliver the cookies to the pushers in black helicopters

Like a lot of complacent Americans, I'll bet you're thinking, "Big deal, I can kick Girl Scout cookies any time I want." I used to think that. Then I'd wake up in a gutter somewhere with a sugar hangover and chocolate smeared around my mouth. Finally, I just couldn't deny it anymore. My name is Mike, and I'm a thin mint-oholic.

My wife tries to get me to quit but to no avail.

"Set the box down and back away from it," she says. "You know you can't eat just one."

I'm sure she means well, but it is hopeless. Besides, I think I might be more inclined to listen to her if she weren't a known abuser of Caramel deLites.

For years, I've gotten my cookies from a connection in the office. A parent would bring in a sign-up sheet, and the next thing I'd know I'd have an empty wallet and a sugar buzz. This year, though, all of the parents said their girls weren't selling cookies. I panicked.

"I don't want to have to buy my stuff on the street," I said. "Who knows how many times those cookies have been stepped on? Somebody must know somebody who is selling."

Sure enough, one of the men had a daughter who knew a girl who might be willing to sell some cookies, provided the price was right. So now I'm $35 poorer, but I have a bodacious cookie stash. I know I'm not the only one, either. Oh, we're happy and bright-eyed now, but there's big trouble for the city on the horizon. Because what do you think will happen when we all run out?

April 4, 1997

TWENTY-TWO

GRADUATION IS THE CHANCE FOR PARENTS TO BASK IN REFLECTED GLORY

It was cool to find my daughter's name in the program under the heading "cum laude." (Yeah, I'm bragging. Sue me.)

Alaska parents don't take real vacations. They accompany their children. They wrestle with cranky toddlers during long airplane rides to grandma's house, where the tots can be properly spoiled. They spend small fortunes to take grade schoolers to theme parks. They force surly adolescents to view natural wonders from the back seats of rental cars. They ferry almost-graduated high schoolers to college campuses. And, if they are lucky, they journey thousands of miles to watch a young adult take a five-second walk across a stage in a mortarboard and gown.

That's where I was two weeks ago. Sitting in a big auditorium on the campus of Pomona College in southern California, grinning like a fool. Nobody noticed. The auditorium was full of parents grinning like fools. As well as grandparents, aunts, uncles, brothers, sisters, friends and classmates. It was a happy crowd.

"The graduates are happy to be finished with college," one of the speakers said, "and the parents are happy to be finished with tuition payments."

Truer words. As I have been telling anyone who would listen, my daughter's college degree is, excepting our house, the most expensive thing we've ever bought. I was fully prepared to express my joy by jumping up and doing the Macarena as she accepted that piece of paper, but the woman who lets me live with her pulled me aside for a quiet word.

"If you are thinking of doing anything to embarrass her during the ceremony," she said, "just remember: It's a long, long walk home."

No longer than the graduation ceremony. I have attended shorter operas. Music. A procession. The national anthem. A prayer. A speech by the college president. Singing. Two speeches by graduating seniors. More singing. Three speeches by alumni receiving honorary degrees. Another speech by the college president. Another procession. Baseball games don't last as long. Extra-inning games. About the time the third honored alumni opened his big yap, I asked the woman who etc. to flag the hot dog vendor the next time she saw him. I still have a bruise where she whacked me with a rolled-up program.

Sandwiched among the pomp and platitudes was the all important moment when each of the 350 or so graduates, from Tabassum Ahmed to Jamie Beth Zadra, received a degree. Amy Kristine Doogan was No. 95.

I'll tell you what was cool about that. It was cool to be on a campus so pretty that film crews roll in from Hollywood every time the shooting script says "college." It was cool to sit among thousands of proud, happy people. It was cool look into the eyes of other parents and know exactly what they were thinking. It was cool to find my daughter's name in the program under the heading "cum laude." (Yeah, I'm bragging. Sue me.) It was cool to bask in the reflected glory of achievement without having to do any of the work. What was cool about this event? Pretty much everything.

I'm tempted to draw some broad conclusion here, as newspaper columnists are paid to do. To say that for every young criminal who makes front page headlines there are hundreds of thousands of young people who work hard and study hard and take their place in the world without any more notice than maybe a paragraph somewhere back around the supermarket ads. That the worst thing they do is wear aqua socks with their robes and toss a beach ball around during the speeches. That on thousands of campuses across the country each year you can find the proof that the world is not growing meaner and darker and more dangerous.

But I won't. Instead, I'll just say that I'm happy and proud, and let that be enough.

MAY 31, 1998

TWENTY-THREE

HOLIDAYS ARE A LITTLE LESS HAPPY THANKS TO BAD CHRISTMAS MUSIC

One reason there is so much bad Christmas music is that there is so much Christmas music. Everybody plays the stuff during the holidays.

When James S. Pierpont published the words and music to "Jingle Bells" in Boston in 1857, I'll bet he never dreamed it would be sung by barking dogs.

Well, it has been, and the result may be the worst Christmas song ever recorded. I say "may be" because it turns out that everyone has a worst Christmas song, and is willing to defend his or her choice in a take-no-prisoners fashion. When I asked my colleagues to tell me what their least-favorite Christmas songs were, a couple of them nearly got into a fistfight over whether the album "James Brown's Funky Christmas" is a blight on the holidays or one of the finest collections of seasonal music ever recorded. And when they began debating a specific song, "Santa Claus Go Straight to the Ghetto," I thought there might be shooting.

Most people think of Christmas music as carols, and most of those songs are, if not loved, at least tolerated. An exception seems to be "The Little Drummer Boy," written in 1941 by Katherine K. Davis. "'Bolero' meets Hallmark," one of my colleagues sniffed. Lots of people hate that song, and I am one of them. In fact, I thought no one could ever do an acceptable version, until I lucked into a recording by Joan Jett and the Blackhearts.

The tolerance most people have doesn't extend to every rendition of the carols, though. Even those not sung by barking dogs. If I never hear Jimmy Durante sing "Frosty the Snowman" again, it'll be too soon. And dyed-in-the-wool Elvis fans agree that the version of "Santa Claus Is Coming to Town" on his Christmas album is not the King's best work.

There is, of course, another category of Christmas music that I'll just call songs. Lots of these songs are really awful. For example, I've often fantasized about getting into a time machine and traveling far enough back to kill Tommie Connor before he could write "I Saw Mommy Kissing Santa Claus" in 1952. Or at least far enough back to strangle Michael Jackson before he could record it. Nobody I talked to could mention Elmo 'n' Patsy's "Grandma Got Run Over by a Reindeer" without gagging, and rude noises also accompanied "One Parent Christmas" by Saffire — The Uppity Blues Women and "I Yust Go Nuts at Christmas," by Yogi Yorgesson.

But real outrage seemed to be reserved for just one group, The Chipmunks. If you haven't heard "The Chipmunk Song" by Simon, Theodore and Alvin, count your blessings. These screechy little rodents began as a DJ's gag and evolved into a cartoon show, proving once again that nobody ever went broke underestimating the taste of the American people. The Chipmunks are so roundly hated by music lovers everywhere that there is a specially revised version of "The Christmas Song," written by Mel Torme and Robert Wells in 1946, that begins: "Chipmunks roasting on an open fire."

One reason there is so much bad Christmas music is that there is so much Christmas music. Everybody plays the stuff during the holidays, and recording artists are not immune to the lure of the fast buck. For every good tune like Chuck Berry's "Run, Run Rudolph," you get a couple of bowzers like "Santa Came Home Drunk" by Clyde Lasley and the Cadillac Baby Specials and "Christmas in Prison" by Doug Legacy and the Legends of the West.

If all of this isn't bad enough, "Jingle Bells" sung by barking dogs has been remixed this year as "Jingle Bell Boogie" sung by barking dogs. And if you're looking for that last-minute gift for someone you really hate, I'm told there are CDs featuring meowing cats and crying babies, too.

Dec. 21, 1997

TWENTY-FOUR

IDITAROD'S ANCHORAGE 'START' IS WHERE MYTH AND MARKETING MEET

Commerce has so come to dominate the race that you can tell who has a chance to win by the number of sponsor insignias he or she wears.

You could hear the dogs for blocks, a cacophony of barks and whines and yelps punctuated by an occasional howl. Five blocks of West Fourth Avenue were outlined in snow fence to keep the crowds at bay. The side streets were lined with fence too. The streets themselves were full of trucked-in snow and dog teams in various states of assemblage and people of all sorts putting dogs into booties or harnesses or just standing around waiting.

Beneath the dogs' dissonant din was a steady hum of human voices. People were everywhere: on the sidewalks along Fourth Avenue and in every window that faced it, en route along Third and Fifth, headed downtown from where they had parked, as far away as the park strip or farther. Lots of families with kids. Lots of cameras. Lots of cardboard cups of coffee held in mittened hands. All come to see an event that exists only at the intersection of myth and marketing.

The Iditarod Trail Sled Dog Race is an event that has almost nothing to do with Alaska's history. Dog teams were not widely used here before whites came. Even during their heyday, most people traveled during summer, when waterways were open. They hunkered down during winter, and when they traveled, they were far more likely to go on snowshoes than by dog team. Dog teams required a lot of food, and people who lived on local resources often couldn't afford to feed them.

The Iditarod has even less to do with American Alaska. The first big rush of immigrants came at the very end of the 19th century. Within 25 years there was a railroad to the Interior. At almost the same time, the first airplanes began flying in northern skies. Even the famous dog sled mail routes lasted only from 1910 to the mid-1930s.

Today's race is not historic in other ways. On established trails, like the short-lived Iditarod Trail, mushers moved from roadhouse to roadhouse. Campouts were caused by miscalculation or misadventure. Everywhere smart travelers sat out bad weather. Only the advent of locator beacons and snowmachine rescuers allowed racers to challenge the fury of nature.

The musher, in short, like the grizzled prospector with his gold pan and the dance hall girl with the heart of gold, exists primarily in the Alaska we wish had been, not the Alaska that was. And the long-distance dog race? Pretty much the creation of Joe Redington's canny promoter's mind.

The Anchorage start is to the race what the race is to Alaska history. The mushers' times between Anchorage and Eagle River are no longer counted, so what organizers call the "restart" in Wasilla is really the start of the race. What happened in Anchorage on Saturday, which organizers call the "ceremonial start," is actually a giant marketing exercise. Lots of people get to see the dogs and racers and sponsors' signs. The crowds make an excellent backdrop for the photos taken by the race and team sponsors. The racers can carry the people who have paid to ride on their sleds without having to worry about times. And the cash registers in Anchorage hotels and restaurants ring and ring and ring.

Commerce has so come to dominate the race that you can tell who has a chance to win by the number of sponsor insignias he or she wears. Even the handlers of last year's winner, Doug Swingley, wore matching jackets sporting a sponsor's logo. Lots of people are anxious to turn myth into money.

But that's the American way. And even a publicity exercise gave lots of people what they wanted: a chance to see the dogs and mushers up close. It was just a circus, but like any circus it was fun.

MARCH 5, 2000

IF A MINER MUST BE AN OPTIMIST, THEN ROGER BURGGRAF QUALIFIES

Burggraf was born in upstate New York, and got interested in rocks when a mining engineer friend of his stepfather sent him a mineral collection from South America.

When the United States government surveyed the 63,592 residents of the territory of Alaska in 1900, it found 7,077 miners and quarrymen, and 579 officials of mining and quarrying companies. In the 100 years since, the population of the state of Alaska has increased almost 10-fold. But, according to state figures, the number of people employed in mining last year was 3,183, less than half of what it was in 1900.

"That's just six Carrs stores," Steve Borell said with a rueful smile.

Borell, executive director of the Alaska Miners Association, was quick to add that a worker at, say, the Red Dog mine is making much better money than a worker at, say, Carrs Aurora Village. But, he said Friday during a break in the association's annual convention and trade show, low prices for gold and other metals have meant that for miners, "It's been really tough."

To be a miner, he said, "You have got to be an optimist."

Roger Burggraf fits that description.

"There's plenty of fish to fry out there," he told a couple of other delegates to the convention, "but you've got to keep your skillet hot."

Burggraf, 69, is a slightly stooped fellow with big shoulders and a soft, friendly voice. Right now, his skillet contains a gold mining operation on Nolan Creek near Wiseman, a coal slurry demonstration project on Ester Dome in Fairbanks and an 86-foot sternwheeled riverboat on the Chena River.

Burggraf was born in upstate New York, and got interested in rocks when a mining engineer friend of his stepfather sent him a mineral collection from South America. But his road to mining was far from straight. He left home at 14 and worked on farms and ranches.

"I worked my way through college waiting tables," he said. He was studying agronomy at Cornell when, for a job one summer, he went to Juneau to work in a mill and "I sort of fell in love with the country." He came back the next summer after other prospects fell through.

"I was going to go down to Guatemala to work for United Fruit Company," Burggraf said, "but they had a revolution and that kind of put a damper on it."

He worked at the dairy in Juneau, decided that was too tame, and got a job as a stream guard with the fish and wildlife service. He was pretty green when a boat set him ashore near Glacier Bay.

"I couldn't figure out why they were in such a hurry to leave," he said. "And then the mosquitoes came in and ate me alive."

Burggraf had to eke out his food with seal liver, had a much-too-close encounter with a brown bear and decided this was the Alaska he wanted to live in. So much so that when he met the woman who would be his first wife, he told her, "If you're not interested in Alaska, you're not interested in me."

After graduating from Cornell with a degree in wildlife management, Burggraf served in the military as an artillery officer, coming back to Alaska in 1959 to take some graduate courses at the university in Fairbanks. He worked in the hotel business, for the electrical utility, as a dog sled freight hauler and as a banker before finally acquiring the gold claim on Ester Dome in the early '70s. He worked on the pipeline while developing the claim, then became a consultant with a bigger concern. Mining's fortunes rose and fell with metals prices, so like a lot of miners he's doing other things as well to make ends meet.

"My wife would like me to retire," he said, "but I'm having too much fun."

Nov. 11, 2001

Twenty-Six

IF THE ELECTION'S AN AUCTION, WHY NOT SPARE VOTERS?

Why go through this long, involved election process, which is nothing more than an equation that reads: Fund raising equals ads equals name identification equals votes?.

The lack of public enthusiasm for next Tuesday's election is proof that we need to improve the way we select officeholders.

For those of you who slept through civics class, our current system is supposed to work like this: Intelligent, accomplished citizens run for office because they want to give something back to their community. Their neighbors help them out and maybe give them a few bucks, while they engage in rational discussion of the issues. The voting populace pays close attention, and on Election Day makes an informed choice. Result: good government.

Our current system really works like this: The odds and ends of society run for office because they want a job with easy hours and good medical and dental. Their neighbors ignore them in the hope they'll go away. Special interests shower them with money, which they pay to consultants and spin doctors, who tell them how to appeal to the lowest common denominator. On Election Day, some fraction of the voting populace sucks it up, goes to the polls, and votes for the names they recognize. Result: the sort of government we have now.

This system keeps a certain number of people off welfare or out of prison. And it allows the well-heeled to stymie fair taxation and regulation while helping themselves from the government purse. So it has an upside. But you can see why some people might want to change it.

Do-gooders think the problem is money. They are always trying to limit the amount that lobbyists and corporations can give. Fortunately, all the judges used to be lawyers, and lawyers seem to know the U.S. Constitution gives our corporate citizens the right to buy politicians, or at least rent them for extended periods.

The lesson here is that, instead of trying to do good, we should be looking out for ourselves. In electoral politics, that means getting out of the middle of the whole mess.

The way the system works now, politicians just won't leave us alone. They spend a lot of money on advertising so we will recognize their names or, if we know their names, to confuse us about what they have been doing in office. These ads are crammed into our favorite TV programs, turning every episode of Jerry Springer into a marathon. Then those of us who feel obligated to behave like good citizens have to traipse off to the polls, where we feel guilty about voting for somebody we wouldn't hire to wash our dog.

Why go through this long, involved election process, which is nothing more than an equation that reads: Fund raising equals ads equals name identification equals votes? Why not just auction off the politicians outright?

That way, we wouldn't have to endure these high-cost, boring campaigns full of lies and evasions. Good for us. The politicians could quit fund raising and concentrate year-round on government-paid junkets. Good for them. Lobbyists and corporations could eliminate the uncertainty of pouring lots of money into a politician who could, at any moment, stumble into the kimchi and drown.

Think of it. No more attack ads, misleading mailers or push polls. No more groups of candidates who look like last call at

Quark's. No more voting with one hand while holding your nose with the other.

There are other benefits. The quality of candidates would improve. Only the candidates who bring in the high bids would win, and nobody is going to bid a bundle on anyone who isn't smart enough to take orders and honest enough to stay bought. That eliminates half the current state House right there. And we could use the income to cut taxes.

So what am I bid on Lot 17, one slightly used state senator without a scrupulous bone in his body? Do I hear fifty-gimmee-fifty-just-fifty ...

AUG. 18, 1998

Twenty-Seven

IF I DROVE AN OSCAR MAYER WIENER, EVERYONE WOULD BE IN LOVE WITH ME

Even with all these extras, the wienermobile has an allure that is as hard to understand as it is to deny. People love the thing.

As you tool around town in a 3-ton wiener, people notice you.

"When you're looking through the windshield of a wiener, people are different," Kevin Burkum said. "You know, it's a side of them that maybe doesn't come out, normally. They've had a rough day, maybe they're not feeling real well, problems at home. They see the wienermobile, and they're happy."

Now, Burkum is supposed to say things like that. For the past 20 months he has been a jeez, I really hate to say this Hotdogger, employed by Oscar Mayer to chauffeur one of the company's six pieces of motorized Pop Art around the country.

But he's right nonetheless. The 23-foot-long, 8-foot-wide, 10-foot-high Fiberglas wiener-on-a-bun-on-wheels is well, dammit, it's charming. I know. I drove it.

The wienermobile is mounted on a 1988 Chevy van chassis and powered by a V- 6 engine. This baby is loaded: power steering, power brakes, microwave oven, telephone, a horn that blares out, among other things, "On, Wisconsin" (Oscar Mayer's home office is in Madison) and a tape player complete with all 21 arrangements of the "I wish I was an Oscar Mayer wiener" song. Every damn one of them.

Rock? Salsa? You name it. Cajun? Rap? You bet. No wonder wienermobiles cost a cool $75,000 per copy.

Even with all these extras, the wienermobile has an allure that is as hard to understand as it is to deny. People love the thing. I pulled up next to a car at the stoplight at 15th and Gambell Monday morning, and the little kid in the back did a double take, grinned and waved. So did the mid-30s man driving. People smile at the wienermobile. And wave. And honk their horn. And flash their lights. And, occasionally, rear-end somebody while they gawk.

"Since we've been in town, we've already caused two fender-benders," said Ann Ela. She is the other Hotdogger accompanying the wienermobile on its first-ever trip to Alaska. Like nuns, Hotdoggers travel in pairs. Unlike nuns, the pairs are usually a man and a woman. Fresh out of college and, if Burkum and Ela are any example, wholesome as, well, hot dogs.

For what Burkum said is "right around $20,000 a year," they pilot wienermobiles from town to town, handing out wienermobile whistles and banks and stickers and watches and T-shirts. The Hotdoggers really, really, really like this job.

"There'll be little things that will happen," Ela said, "like you'll be driving along and an ambulance will come screeching by you. And the person will sit up from their stretcher and look out the window and wave at you. That's happened to me."

Yeah, I know. But would a fresh-faced young person wearing a bright orange shirt with a wienermobile logo right in the middle of the chest lie to you?

The wienermobile is here because Oscar Mayer is sponsoring two teams in the Iditarod. (No, they won't be pulled by wiener dogs.) The company spends more than $1 million a year to keep the six vehicles and 13 Hotdoggers on the road and to keep them in gee-gaws.

"Those whistles aren't cheap, they cost 16 cents apiece," Burkum said as Ela drove down Northern Lights. "And we give them out by the thousands. Nobody wants just one."

I could see why. Evidence of the wienermobile's appeal was all around us. People on the sidewalk waved and pointed. A pickup truck full of waving people passed. In the back was the most surprised-looking dog I've ever seen. In the next lane, a man drove with one hand while trying to shoot a picture of the wienermobile over his shoulder with the other.

Like I said, as you tool around town in a 3-ton wiener, people notice you.

FEB. 26, 1991

TWENTY-EIGHT

IF IT'S GOOD ENOUGH FOR THE KENNEDYS, WHY NOT TRY AUCTION HERE?

I don't know about your garage, but my garage looks like the lost-and-found at U-Haul.

Let me tell you why I didn't clean out my garage this weekend.

To begin with, I had other chores. Just raking the gravel out of my yard took half a day. Then I raked up the last of the fall leaves and the winter kill, inhaling the dust that stirred up, and sneezing. I got a nice little rhythm going: rake, rake, rake, sneeze; rake, rake, rake, sneeze. Before I knew it, neighborhood kids were break-dancing in my driveway.

The dust and gravel come from the streets. Between them, anybody who owns property has become an unpaid part of the city workforce. The city puts the stuff down, we pick it up. We pay them to put it down. They don't pay us to pick it up. What's wrong with this picture?

My wife was unsympathetic to this complaint.

"If you want to storm city hall with a mob of angry, rake-wielding property owners, fine," she said. "But not until you've finished your chores."

So I did what any hard-working, property-owning husband would have done in my situation. I took a coffee break.

"Wake up," my wife said, shaking me. "And turn off that basketball game. It's time to clean the garage."

I don't know about your garage, but my garage looks like the lost-and-found at U-Haul. It contains old furniture and appliances, hoses, rakes, extension cords, pieces of wood that might come in handy some day, shovels, three ladders, PVC pipe, a barbecue grill, motor oil, automotive tools, sports equipment, and a bunch of stuff I've never seen before in my life. Cleaning it would be no day at the beach.

"I'm not ready to clean the garage yet," I said. "I haven't been able to get a date from Sotheby's."

My wife gave me that special look women use when a man is behaving even more stupidly than normal.

"Sotheby's?" she asked. "Just what's in that coffee cup?"

"Look," I said, rubbing my eyes, "we've got to get rid of all that stuff."

"I know," she said. "I thought we'd have a garage sale."

I snorted.

"That just shows how little attention you pay to current events," I said. "Do you think the Kennedy kids would have gotten $211,500 for their mother's fake pearls if they'd been selling them off a card table in the driveway? Heck, no. The only way to make real money on old junk is an auction."

By the time I finished talking, my wife was shaking her head.

"That wasn't just anybody's old junk," she said. "That was John and Jackie Kennedy's old junk. People were willing to pay a lot of money to be able to say they own something that used to belong to the Kennedys. But why would they pay a lot of money for your old junk?"

"I know I don't have the Kennedy mystique," I said. "But I don't have the Kennedy overhead, either. Somebody paid $772,500 for Jack Kennedy's old golf clubs. I've got some old tennis rackets and a softball bat. If I could get just 1 percent of what the golf clubs brought, I'd be happy. Don't you think I could?"

"Well," my wife said. "the way you hit, the softball bat is practically brand new. But I just don't think you're being very realistic."

"Me?" I said. "I'm not the one being unrealistic. The bidders are. Somebody paid $12,650 for bundles of old magazines. I've got old magazines. Why shouldn't I strike while the bidding fever is hot?"

My wife rolled her eyes and gave up. So I got through the weekend without having to clean the garage. Not that that was my goal, mind you. Certainly not. I've still got hopes of hearing from those people at Sotheby's. I might not get $34.5 million for my old junk, but I might raise enough to hire somebody to do the yard work next spring.

APRIL 30, 1996

Twenty-Nine

IF YOU LIKED 'DANCES WITH WOLVES,' YOU'LL LOVE 'TALKS WITH ANIMALS'

All of this has turned animal telepathy into what can only be called Smith's profession. But she says her efforts are motivated by a lot more than commerce.

I asked my wife's cats what they thought about Penelope Smith. As usual, they just sat there, looking smug and superior. That's the difference between me and Smith. I talk to animals. She says animals talk to her.

"Basically, I've communicated with animals all my life," Smith said Tuesday, "been aware of it, that I could do it, and that I could understand them and get their thoughts and their feelings."

In fact, Smith, who lives in Point Reyes, Calif. yes, that's in Marin County makes her living talking to animals and teaching other people to talk to them. She is an animal telepath. Full time. Honest to God. She says business is booming.

"Right now I'm in the midst of writing a book, a new book, so I've cut down my consultations and turned them over to my assistants, the people I've trained. But I literally could be full time on the phone night and day, with the amount of calls I get."

The book will be her second about communicating with animals. You can still buy the first, "Animal Talk," as well as four audio tapes and a videotape. There is also a newsletter, "Species Link," and her lectures, workshops and consultations, some in person and some over the telephone. Not that Smith needs the telephone. You do.

A busy schedule, but not too busy to prevent business travel. Last month it was Toronto. This month, this weekend in fact, it's Anchorage. A public lecture tonight, a two-day workshop day one without your animal friend (these people don't say "pet") and day two with and consultations by appointment.

All of this has turned animal telepathy into what can only be called Smith's profession. But she says her efforts are motivated by a lot more than commerce.

"I help people to get back their ability to telepathically communicate with other species. . . . My main purpose in doing this is to help, actually it's a planetary purpose, to help people to get back in touch so that we don't destroy it all, so that we don't lose it all. Because our separation and our use of other species has caused our decline, and the destruction of the planet that we're experiencing now."

I think it was about here that I decided not to ask Smith if she owned a fur coat. But I did ask her why people would give up the ability to communicate with animals if, as she said, everybody was born with it.

"Our culture has been geared for several hundred years to separating humans from the rest of nature," she said. "When we turned to industrializing, when we turned to the scientific approach of looking at others as objects, we ended up losing the spiritual connection and divorcing ourselves from the rest of nature."

Ah, those twin devils, industrialization and the scientific method. I might have known.

There's that other devil, reporter skepticism, chiming in.

Alex Kochkin, a local pollster and the man responsible for Smith's trip to Anchorage, was kind of worried about that. Actually, he seemed really worried about that. So he loaned me a videotape full of normal-looking people who explained in normal-sounding voices that Smith had talked to their animals and helped them deal with their emotional baggage. Unfortunately, the tape ended before any of the people revealed the details of Elvis' comeback tour.

See? Some beings just aren't as evolved as others. Smith knows that.

"I have so many people who are open and who learn from this and whose lives are benefitted from it, that those who are skeptical can do their thing," she said. "I don't really run into too many (unbelieving) people, except of course reporters and people like that, whose business is to be skeptical."

Skeptical? Moi? You think I'm skeptical, you should talk to these cats.

Aug. 9, 1991

THIRTY

JUNEAU WOMAN WORKS TO HEAL 'RAW, OPEN WOUND' OF DWI TRAGEDY

Ladd Macaulay's death was a blow to Juneau. So many people showed up for his funeral that speakers had to be set up outside the church. But the damage was greatest in his family.

The family was going to go camping at the Shrine of Saint Terese, out past Lemon Creek and Auke Bay and Tee Harbor on the only road worth mentioning in Juneau.

"We were all excited, but Dad was probably most excited of all," said Cindy Cashen. "He always loved it when we got together."

Cashen's dad, Ladd Macaulay, worked in the state Department of Community and Economic Development. Along with his boss and a biologist from Fish and Game, he was inspecting remote fish hatcheries on the Kenai Peninsula. He was supposed to drive back to Anchorage and catch the flight to Juneau that night, April 19.

"I was getting ready for bed, and I got a phone call," Cashen said, "and it was the policeman on the phone, and he advised me to come to my mother's house."

Cashen lives in downtown Juneau. Her parents live out on the road. She had plenty of time to worry on the drive.

"I was God-bargaining the whole way out," she said. "You know. God, don't let it be anything bad and I'll never swear again."

Most everything in Juneau is either up a set of stairs or down a set of stairs. Her parents' house, on the beach, is down a long stairway. Cashen remembers walking down those stairs saying "Oh, God" with every step.

When she reached the house, "it was dark and I heard someone sobbing and it was my mom and she got up and started walking towards me and I said, 'Mom, what's wrong?' and she said, 'Dad's been killed by a drunk driver.'"

Macaulay and his boss, Martin John Richard, died on the Seward Highway when their rental car was hit by a pickup. The driver, Michael J. Glaser, had a blood-alcohol level of at least .258 at the time of the wreck, according to state troopers. He has been charged with two counts of second-degree murder for their deaths and first-degree assault for injuries to Fish and Game biologist Steven Gregory McGee. The wreck was the first in our recent string of disasters caused by suspected drunken drivers.

Macaulay's death was a blow to Juneau. He was a local boy who graduated from high school there. The policemen who came to tell his wife of his death had learned baseball from him. So many people showed up for his funeral that speakers had to be set up outside the church. But the damage was greatest in his family: his wife, Linda, and their four children, Cashen, her sister, and their two brothers. Part of Cashen's response to her father's death is activism. She is trying to start a chapter of Mothers Against Drunk Driving in Juneau.

"This is how I'm grieving," she said. "I'd be in a loony bin if I wasn't able to do something."

MADD has a rule that a victim can't start a chapter for a year. So the Juneau organization would actually be part of the Anchorage chapter until the year is up. Cashen says the group will work to educate people about drunken driving and lobby the state Legislature about funding, programs and policies related to the issue. Juneau, she says, has a drunken driving problem even though it doesn't have that many streets. The town actually has more drunken driving arrests per capita than Anchorage, with arrests for driving while intoxicated an almost daily event.

"You wouldn't believe some of the DWIs we get," she said. "They could have walked home."

But the diversion of organizing the MADD chapter is only part of the process Cashen is going through. We tend to think of the victims of drunken drivers as the people they kill and injure. But the damage extends far beyond that.

"It's a very raw, open wound," Cashen said of her father's death. "And every time a scab forms, something happens to open it up again. Even the wonderful things — they named the salmon derby after him — those rip that scab open."

"This one choice, this one stupid choice this guy made. It's like a ripple in a pond. It's never going to end."

July 7, 2000

Thirty-One

KNOWLES EMBARRASSES ALASKA TO ADVANCE HIS POLITICAL CAREER

The fact is, Tony, it's you who ought to be consulting with Alaskans on oil policy, not Carter. He's a private citizen, remember?

An open letter to Gov. Tony Knowles

Dear Gov. Knowles:

I read with some amazement the "open letter" you wrote to former President Jimmy Carter. It has long been clear to everyone in Alaska that everything you say and do is a matter of political calculation. But the way you handled your differences with Carter on drilling in the Arctic National Wildlife Refuge is an embarrassment to Alaskans. We don't need you to embarrass us, Tony. We have Don Young for that.

First, there's the fiction of the "letter."

You didn't send Carter a letter, Tony. You wrote a press release. If the "letter" had been intended for Carter, you would have seen to it that he got it before you released it to the press. But you didn't. He might have had it for all of 15 minutes before you started the press conference that you'd called just to hand out the "letter" to every newspaper and TV and radio station you could persuade to attend.

So clearly your "letter" wasn't written to try to convince Carter of anything. It was written to get you in front of the TV cameras acting tough. Well, I suppose that if you want to lead the mob, you have to shout louder and caper more grotesquely than the next demagogue.

Then there's the content of the "letter."

You chastise Carter for not having "any meaningful dialogue with the people of Alaska."

That's rich, coming from you. Remind me: How much meaningful dialogue did you have with the people of Alaska before you did a deal with BP on the Northstar field? You remember that deal, don't you? The one in which you gave away millions of dollars in state revenue?

You were just as anxious to hear what the public had to say about your support of BP's acquisition of Arco, weren't you? That's why you held a rushed set of hearings after you'd already done a deal with BP.

And then there are the extensive public hearings you've held to determine the state's position on drilling in ANWR.

The fact is, Tony, it's you who ought to be consulting with Alaskans on oil policy, not Carter. He's a private citizen, remember? You're supposed to be a public official.

But the absolute best part of the "letter" is where you accuse Carter of using Alaska "as a media prop and platform."

How many times do you suppose you have traveled at state expense to pose in front of some convenient prop to announce a program or sign a bill? Here's Tony at the Whittier tunnel. There's Tony at the Mendenhall Glacier. You've spent so much time posing in front of the kids at Denali Elementary they think you're their teacher.

You lecturing Carter for using Alaska as a prop is like Jennifer Lopez lecturing somebody for dressing trashy.

Here's something else to think about. Maybe if you'd talked with Carter before he gave his speech, you might have actually had some impact on him. But according to your spokesman Bob King, you were too busy. Doing what? Well, King said, on the day of Carter's speech, you "named a new commissioner of public safety, opened the cargo summit in Girdwood, dedicated a plaque to the railroad worker killed during last winter's avalanches and then flew on to Kodiak to meet with fishermen on the Steller sea lion issue."

Now, that's some heavy lifting. I can see how you couldn't squeeze an ex-president of the United States into a schedule like that. But it does make me wonder how you can claim Carter abused his welcome, since you didn't offer him one.

The truth is nobody's buying any of this. We all know that you're just trying to position yourself for the next step up the ladder of your ambition. You figure the environmentalists will have to support you because they don't have anywhere else to go. And you figure taking cheap shots at Carter will put you in even more solid with the good old boys in the oil patch.

You know, Tony, you really ought to be ashamed of yourself for behaving so shabbily. But I guess you're past that.

Aug. 27, 2000

Thirty-Two

THE LAST TRIP TO THE VET'S IS A DIFFICULT AND MELANCHOLY JOURNEY

The cat had always been a bad patient. Cats don't like being handled, and this one was named Spook in part because she was afraid of strangers.

Writers have a private way to prepare for life's difficulties. They imagine what they will write afterward. I sat thinking about what would happen and how I would feel about it and how I would describe everything. I tried to build a wall of words to keep the events of the next hour at a safe distance. When the time came, I took the pet carrier in and set it on the bed. I slid open the closet doors, reached down and picked up the orange-and-white cat. I turned and handed her into the carrier, then fastened the wire mesh door. I did all this quickly. Given the chance, the cat would make putting her into the carrier as difficult and painful as juggling chain saws.

I am not a cat fancier. They are aloof and destructive. I am allergic to them. But this cat had been with us for more than 10 years. I'd grown attached to her. Most nights, the last thing I did before I went to bed was scratch her head and discuss the day's events.

As I drove, I talked with the cat and chewed on a toothpick. The cat emitted a string of plaintive, I-don't-like-this meows. Then she made the noise she'd taken to making when something hurt her mouth.

She'd been making the noise more often lately, as the cancer spread. Antibiotics could control the infections that accompanied it, but nothing could stop the cancer. The antibiotics, used too often, would cause kidney failure. The only pain killer strong enough to do any good would kill the cat.

She lost weight, slept more, dragged. As she got worse, our choices vanished. A couple of nights earlier, she'd hurt herself eating, running away as if the pain was in her dish and not her mouth. My wife and I decided we'd waited as long as we could. She just couldn't take the cat to the vet this time, she said. Could I?

The people at the vet's office were kind and efficient. I paid and signed a form saying I knew why we were all there. They put the cat and me in a small room with a waist-high metal table. The vet and an assistant came in. The vet explained again in her gentle voice that I could just leave the cat with them if I wanted. I shook my head. I didn't think it was right that the cat should go through this among strangers.

The cat had always been a bad patient. Cats don't like being handled, and this one was named Spook in part because she was afraid of strangers. The vet explained that she would give Spook a tranquilizer, to make what was to come easier for everyone. She did, then said they'd be back in five minutes. I stroked Spook and talked with her. She grew calm and wobbly. She lay down. The toothpick was just bits of wood in my mouth.

The vet and her assistant came back in. The vet shaved Spook's right front paw. The assistant blocked the vein. The vet picked up a syringe. I looked away from where the needle bit the skin and watched her push the plunger home.

Spook put her head down and died.

Death came so quickly and quietly that it took me a few moments to realize Spook was gone. The vet checked for a heartbeat. There was none. She looked in the corpse's mouth, and assured me once again that we had done the right thing, the humane thing.

In the car, I reminded myself it was just a cat. But it wasn't. One of the things that makes us human is that, for better and worse, our reason does not always inform our emotions. We know in our heads that the deaths of thousands of people on the other side of the planet are the real tragedy, but it is for the cat we held in our arms that we grieve in our hearts.

AUG. 8, 1994

THIRTY-THREE

LAW SAYS A BIRD IS NOT AN ANIMAL, SO MARIE CAN KEEP ON HONKING

Marie, she said, does not honk incessantly. True, two summers ago, he might have been honking a lot at other neighbors who were building a shed.

Marie is a goose. A gander, actually.

"He's a proud and elegant goose," said his owner, Dr. Jeanne Bonar. "And handsome."

Marie lives, along with a chicken and three ducks, in the back yard of Bonar's home in College Village. They live there year-round.

"Occasionally," Bonar said, "when it gets very cold, I'll bring the chicken into the garage, because her comb gets frostbitten."

But a frostbitten chicken isn't Bonar's problem. Marie is. Marie honks too much. At least that's what Bonar's next-door neighbor, Roger Marks, says.

"There's one goose that is particularly loud," Marks said. "Anytime you go into the back yard, it just screams at you for hours."

So Marks complained. At first, he complained to Bonar, who, he said, was courteous and responsive. But, he said, nothing quieted Marie.

Finally, he said, "(Bonar) consulted a veterinarian about having it dehonked, and apparently the veterinarian said that would be inhumane."

So Marks complained to the city. One place he complained was the zoning department. The zoning code enforcement office decided that Bonar was, indeed, violating the code, because

(a) Marie is not a dog, (b) the zoning code requires that "paddocks, stables or similar structures or enclosures which are utilized for the keeping of animals other than dogs shall be at least 100 feet from any lot line" and (c) Bonar's fence, a "similar enclosure," is not "at least 100 feet from any lot line." So, (d) Marie must go.

A whole lot of who-shot-John ensued. Eventually, because of a paperwork glitch, the issue ended up in the lap of hearing officer R. Stanley Ditus.

"It is apparent that the word 'animal,'" he wrote Nov. 14, "as used in the land use code means a mammal as distinguished from a bird, reptile or other non-mammal."

In other words, Marie can stay. And the city can't take away your dream of using your back yard to ranch emus.

"Or alligators," said Marks, "because they're not animals."

Bonar said she hopes the decision will put an end to what she sees as the persecution of Marie.

"We've had four hearings this summer, since June," she said. "I'm very distressed by it."

Marie, she said, does not honk incessantly. True, two summers ago, he might have been honking a lot at other neighbors who were building a shed. And he might honk once in a while for neighborhood children who feed him. But he doesn't honk all the time. Besides, she said, she measured Marie's honk on a decibel meter and it is not nearly as loud as an average dog's bark. So she has no intention of getting rid of Marie, who she believes to be the only goose on earth with a brick in Town Square.

"He shares it with a dove and a chicken," she said.

Even though he didn't mention the brick, Marks knows he's dealing with a bird fancier.

"This doctor has footprints of chickens in the sidewalk in front of her house," he said.

Marks said he's waiting for the next verdict on Marie, due out any day from the city's animal control office. If that goes against him, he isn't sure what he'll do.

"Actually, what I want to do is throw a pit bull over her fence," he said. Clearly, the honking has gotten to him.

"If your neighbor has a dog, he learns who you are in about three days," Marks said. "I guess if you have a brain the size of a lima bean, you don't learn much."

Just as clearly, this sort of talk distresses Bonar.

"No matter what you write about the situation," she said, "please be kind to Marie. Because he's a dearly loved goose."

Nov. 23, 1994

THIRTY-FOUR

LEGAL SYSTEM PROVIDES SCANT JUSTICE IN LITTLE BOY'S BEATING DEATH

*Hard to see that as the right outcome. Hard for me and,
I suspect, hard for the letter writer.*

The letter arrived in August, I think. It was neatly typed, and told a simple story. A 2-year-old boy named Kyle Blanchard had been beaten to death the previous October. The writer was a member of the same Air Force unit as the child's mother, Melissa, and her boyfriend, Richard Pommenville, who had been charged with second-degree murder.

The writer was uneasy about the investigation of Kyle's death, and what had happened since, and had several questions: Why was it taking so long for Pommenville's trial to start? Why was he running around loose in the meantime? Why hadn't the mother been charged?

Assistant District Attorney Kevin Fitzgerald, who handled the case in its early stages, had answers. Pommenville's case was set for trial Nov. 15. The time between Kyle's murder and the trial wasn't unusually long.

"I usually figure a rough estimate on murder cases now at a year," he said.

Pommenville was out on bail, with a third-party custodian, and assurances that if he ran, the military would help the state catch him and bring him back.

"With respect to the mother," Fitzgerald said, "that was a really difficult choice."

Melissa Blanchard did not admit hitting Kyle and refused to testify in Pommenville's trial, instead asserting her Fifth Amendment right against self-incrimination.

"There were all sorts of very difficult decisions and choices being made at that time," Fitzgerald said. "We decided that we just didn't have enough evidence to charge her."

I let it go at that. The case finally went to trial last week. It ended when the state's case fell apart and prosecutor Mary Anne Henry agreed to a plea bargain of third-degree assault, normally the charge for hurting someone just a little, or just threatening someone.

The prosecution had theorized that Kyle was killed by blows to the head. Pommenville had confessed to hitting Kyle in the head. But an expert witness for the defense convinced Henry that body blows killed Kyle. Nobody had confessed to hitting the little boy in the body.

Henry sounded glum the day after her decision.

"I just figured, it looks like I'm going to lose the murder case, and I want to get something out of this," she said.

But, I said, wasn't it clear that one of two people had killed the boy?

"That's right," she said. "From what we can tell, one or both of them is responsible."

Then why not just charge them both and let the jury sort it out?

"Under our ethics, we can't. We should not file charges unless we feel that we can convince 12 reasonable people beyond a reasonable doubt," Henry said.

"Based on the current status of the evidence, there's not enough to convict either one of them. And if we can't convict, we can't charge them."

It took some guts for Henry to make that decision. If nothing else, she could have laid off the problem on the jury. In the long view, taking into account the integrity of the legal system and the fundamental idea that everyone is innocent until proven guilty, her decision was probably the right one.

But in the short view, the view focused on the body of Kyle Blanchard?

"Nobody's going to be held responsible for the murder," Henry said.

Hard to see that as the right outcome. Hard for me and, I suspect, hard for the letter writer. Hard for anyone looking into the legal system from the outside. Hard to understand how one dead little boy and two suspects adds up to a maximum sentence of a year in jail.

"It's difficult to explain," Henry said.

More like impossible, I'd say.

Dec. 13, 1994

THIRTY-FIVE

THE LIVES OF OUR MOTHERS ARE MORE THAN TAKING CARE OF CHILDREN

*She kept working after she married my father and moved to Fairbanks.
Alaska wasn't much for stay-at-home wives in those days.*

My mother is shrinking. Not that she was ever very tall — I think her imagination is standing on tiptoe when she claims to have been 5-foot-2 once — but 82 years of gravity have compacted her to less than 5 feet. Her hair grays a little more each year. Her voice is developing the quaver I associate with old age. She moves more slowly, too, but that is mostly due to the spare parts she has had installed: a knee, followed by a hip. She really alarms airport metal detectors now, but she has kept her sense of humor about it.

"I'm not sure about investing this much money in an old chassis," she said before she had the hip replaced.

Those joints got plenty of use before she traded them in. I have a picture of her as a teenage member of the high school girls basketball team in Skagway, where she was born. Another at 21, posing with some pals on a ski outing in Juneau, when she was working for the federal game commission in what is now the Capitol Building. She kept working after she married my father and moved to Fairbanks. Alaska wasn't much for stay-at-home wives in those days. She worked first for the business they ran, then for the state Department of Labor there and, later, here.

But I'm sure most of the wear and tear came from having children. Pregnancies. Childbirths. Chasing six kids around. I'm surprised she has any of her original joints left. Or any sense of humor, for that matter.

I suppose it's because she comes from a long line of determined and independent women. Her father's mother was widowed young, when her husband fell off a horse and died on the White Pass Trail. She raised five children on her own. Her own mother was a typesetter at a Skagway newspaper and ran a gift shop. After she retired and her husband died, she wore a red wig and bombed around Southern California at a steady 45 mph in an immaculate 1954 Ford.

My mother doesn't drive. The family story is that she asked my father to teach her, but he criticized her technique during the first lesson and she refused to get behind the wheel again. That is not the only story that highlights what some people might call her stubbornness. As newlyweds, she and my father lived in a tent in the gold fields outside Fairbanks. One day, she decided to bake an apple pie, and despite the drawbacks of using a woodstove and having absolutely no experience as a baker, she did. My father took a bite, screwed up his face, and told her that she had forgotten the sugar. When he told the story, he said this very mildly. When she tells it, he barked at her. She responded by hurling the pie, pan and all, out of the tent. They were married for 56 years, until he died last year, and she never baked another pie.

Today is the day we remember our mothers. I could have written something about all the things mine did for me. Instead, I decided to remember her in a different way. Each of our mothers has her own story, a life she lived before we arrived in her home and after we left and all the time we were there. Their mothers had such stories, too, and their mothers and so on back into the mists of history. There is more to them than all the meals they fed us, sicknesses they nursed us through and worrying they did about us. There's no greeting card that says this, but it's a good day to remember it anyway.

MAY 10, 1998

THIRTY-SIX

LOOK! IN THE SKY! IT'S A BIRD! IT'S A PLANE! NO, IT'S (STILL) DADMAN!

Three days later, the phone rang. It was our daughter. They were in Fort Nelson, B.C. The car had blown a head gasket.

Helping raise two children taught me a lot of lessons. Don't toss the baby in the air right after he's eaten. Always check the backs of their hands, too. Making them listen to your old Beach Boys records won't improve their musical taste. The list goes on and on. In fact, I learned another one just a couple of weeks ago: You never quit being a parent.

Now, you're probably saying to yourself just what I said when I had this blinding insight: Well, duh. But the truth is, I'd always thought of being a parent as a job. You put in your time, retire, and take up golf. Your children go off, fashion their adult lives, and take their own places in the assembly line as parents. Hopefully, they spend part of their time hanging out with you, but you don't have to cut their meat for them. In fact, if you live long enough, they end up cutting your meat for you. But that's a different story.

So when our daughter turned 21 and graduated from college, I thought that was that. One more summer at home and she'd be off to start the rest of her life. Since there was a rumor going around that our son was, any month now, going to move out of the basement, I'd be able to quit buying college credits and gallons of milk and start buying Tiger Woods instructional videos and plus fours.

Over the summer, our daughter decided for certain that she wanted to go to law school.

"It's the big one!" I cried, clutching my chest. "I'm coming to join you, Elizabeth!"

Don't worry, she told me. I'm going to go to California, work, and establish residency. It'll cost a lot less.

Two weeks ago, she set off to do just that. She and her boyfriend stuffed his '85 Ford station wagon with clothes and books and camping gear. After making sure they had a spare tire and a full roll of duct tape, we bid them adieu.

The woman who lets me live with her was a little blue after they left.

"C'mon," I said, "watch this tape on short irons with me. That'll cheer you up."

I definitely felt different. You're no longer Dadman, fixer of problems and writer of checks, I told myself. You're just another incredibly hip 50-year-old with a wicked hitch in his backswing.

Three days later, the phone rang. It was our daughter. They were in Fort Nelson, B.C. The car had blown a head gasket.

I immediately went into full fatherhood mode. Checked the map. Sure enough, right in the middle of nowhere. Began calculating how long it would take me, or at least enough money to solve this problem, to get to Fort Nelson, all the while firing off questions in Dad-interrogates-4-year-old style.

Our daughter was very cool about the whole thing. No, they didn't need help. She was just checking in. The trip would continue, although they'd be in Fort Nelson a while.

"You know," the woman who lets me live with her said when I put down the phone, "she is 21."

I did know. I had, in fact, been celebrating that. But somehow all my theorizing hadn't gotten down to wherever parenthood lives. When I thought about it, I realized I would, in some way that is beyond my control, always be Dadman.

I realized something else, too. All those times my own parents offered help or gave advice, they weren't, as I thought then, meddling. They were just being parents. Probably couldn't help themselves either.

I explained all this to the woman who lets me live with her. She just smiled and patted me on the head.

"If you keep your elbows in closer, Sparky," she said, "your backswing will smooth right out."

SEPT. 13, 1998

THIRTY-SEVEN

MALONE PUT THE GOOD OF ALASKA, AND OPEN PUBLIC PROCESS, FIRST

He forged these policies not, as is the practice today, behind closed doors, but in long meetings and hearings full of expert testimony and sharp debate.

There's an image I have of Hugh Malone from the late 1970s, sitting at a committee table in a hopelessly out-of-style sports coat, his thin, pale face topped by an unruly mop of already graying hair, listening to something being murmured by a sleek, white-haired investment banker in $500 worth of gray pinstripes.

If this had been anyplace else but Alaska, and any other time but then, he would not have been listening to a Wall Street sharpie. Malone was a working class guy, a surveyor. He had an abiding suspicion of institutions and the people who run them. Most of us are, one way or another, our parents' children, so I always figured he'd inherited that from his father, Frank, who carried the outrages of the British against him and his Irish kinsmen forever fresh upon his lips.

There was a lot to Malone that is, to me still, mysterious. To others as well; in the days since word of his accidental death while on vacation in Italy reached here, several people, some of whom knew him much better than I, have called him an enigma. So I don't know just where he, a high school dropout, acquired such an abiding faith in knowledge. Or where he found the monumental patience that allowed him to listen to both the wise and the foolish for as long as it took.

These are the things that Malone brought to politics, first on the Kenai Peninsula, then for 12 years, from 1973 to his retirement in

1984, in the state House of Representatives. These things and a few more: intelligence, a flinty resolve to do right by the people of Alaska, and a sense of the world that was, in the end, perfectly Irish, in the way described to the *New York Times* by the writer William Kennedy:

"'I was staying at the Gresham Hotel, and the weather was perfect. I commented to a bellboy about the beautiful day, and he replied, "Two more days of this and everyone will be praying for rain."'

"Mr. Kennedy chuckled. 'Somebody told me once that this trait is built into the Irish. They can't take too much good fortune. Rain is their natural condition.'"

Malone rose to prominence in the Legislature as Alaska, a place poor in material goods, was expecting billions in oil revenue. What a time it was. The possibilities seemed limitless, exceeded only by the schemes of those who hoped to enrich themselves by plundering the public purse. As Finance Committee chairman, then House speaker, Malone concerned himself first with getting the state its fair share of the oil revenue, then with preserving some of it for a rainy day in the Alaska Permanent Fund.

He forged these policies not, as is the practice today, behind closed doors, but in long meetings and hearings full of expert testimony and sharp debate. These deliberations used to drive his political opponents, and sometimes his allies, mad with frustration, but he believed that the right process would yield the right result. When that result was higher oil taxes, angering the powers in the oil patch part of his district, he stuck to it anyway, enduring several close elections as a result.

Malone will, no doubt, be missed by many people in many ways. As a state, we will miss his devotion to an open public process and a set of priorities that put all of Alaska always first. We would have wished him a longer life, but not a longer political career. It is as hard to imagine him in the Legislature of today as it is to imagine Gulliver among the Lilliputians.

MARCH 16, 2001

THIRTY-EIGHT

MAYBE WHAT MAKES AN ALASKAN IS AS SIMPLE AS LOVING ALASKA

I've met people who live in Alaska who don't seem to be Alaskans. People can live here for a long time with one foot on the airplane.

Some readers reacted to my question about what makes a real Alaskan with one line.

"A real Alaskan sticks with it through boom and bust!" wrote someone I know only by the nom de net of "goatbert."

Some reacted with an eruption of one-liners.

"You know you're an Alaskan when you only have three spices — salt, pepper, ketchup," wrote Franklin Gatlin. "You design your Halloween costumes to fit over snowsuits. . . . You have more miles on your snowblower than on your car. . . . The most effective mosquito repellent is a .410 shotgun. . . . You know which kinds of leaves make the best toilet paper. . . . The four seasons are: Winter, Still Winter, Not Winter and Almost Winter."

He had lots more, but you get the idea.

S.M. Culhane sent in an 85-item list, many of them borrowed from others. Here's one from that list I've always liked: "You are vacationing in Hawaii when a beautiful woman in a bikini walks by and you think, 'Boy, I'd sure like to see her in a snowmachine suit.'"

As regular readers know, I've been searching for a new definition of what makes someone an Alaskan. For most of my life, the formula was simple: The longer you'd lived here, the more Alaskan you were. But since life here has gotten so much easier, how long you've lived here no longer seems like an adequate test. So I asked for other ways of figuring Alaskanness.

A few people thought things you don't do make you an Alaskan.

"Real Alaskans accept the weather w/o comment," wrote Barbara Landi.

"An Alaskan should not whine and cry for assistance when their power goes out for a few days," Rob and Kim Raum-Suryan wrote, "they should have the ingenuity to get by on their own."

But most of those who responded located Alaskanness in attitudes rather than actions.

"I myself feel it's the spirit of wilderness . . . the wild within a person that truly makes them an Alaskan," Robert Algeri wrote. "I've met people living in the Lower 48 that possessed this spirit, and I've also met people living in Alaska that didn't possess this attribute."

I've met people who live in Alaska who don't seem to be Alaskans. People can live here for a long time with one foot on the airplane. But I don't think what makes them not Alaskans is their attitude toward wilderness. And I think it's stretching things just a skosh too far to think that an attitude — any attitude — can make you an Alaskan if you don't live here. I can understand why Algeri might advance such a thesis, though. He lives in Nashua, N.H.

Joann Budka sent an e-mail message from Copper Center in which she invoked a different attitude, the one of "take care of it yourself."

"Many years ago, north of Copper Center, I witnessed the aftermath of a minor accident," she wrote. "In 15 minutes' time, the passengers were on their way to a clinic with a passerby, the damaged vehicles were off the road, and the glass had been swept off the pavement — all before the troopers probably even heard of the accident. Whether one has lived here four weeks or 40 years, it seems that attitude is the defining element of the true

Alaskan. Those that go on by when they could have helped are never going to make it."

That's more in line with my way of thinking. An Alaskan is concerned more about other people than wilderness, and as much about others as about himself. That would mean that there are a lot of people living here who aren't Alaskans, but then that's the way it's always been.

But I could be wrong. At least one reader, Kim Kowalski-Rogers of Seward, thinks I'm just overcomplicating matters.

"How silly you all are," she wrote, "a true Alaskan simply loves Alaska."

FEB. 15, 2000

NAMING DEAD IS SOMETHING BAGOY 'ALWAYS FELT HAD TO BE DONE'

For the past 14 years, he's been working to restore the cemetery and put names to some 3,000 unmarked graves.

Community is a word that gets thrown around a lot these days. We use it to describe ethnic groups, pieces of the city, government programs. But its true meaning lies elsewhere, in the general sense that we all share in a social order that is held together by a web of benefits and responsibilities.

That sense of community is sometimes hard to come by in Anchorage. People come and go. While they are here, too many put their own desires or convenience above the common good. But if you know where to look, you can find some people who are weaving the web instead of unraveling it. At 11 a.m. tomorrow, at Anchorage Memorial Park Cemetery, the Cook Inlet Historical Society will honor one of those people, John Bagoy.

Bagoy is a rarity, an old-timer who was born here. His family name still adorns the florist business his parents started not long after moving here from the twin cities of Iditarod and Flat. Bagoy was born here in 1922, attended Anchorage schools, had his college interrupted by World War II, finished it after the war and came back. He worked for most of his career as a peddler, as he describes it, selling electrical equipment.

Sitting over coffee with him at City Market last week, I could see how he would have been a successful salesman. He's a guy who knows how to shoot the breeze. And he's got a few stories to tell.

He can tell you how, during Prohibition, the bootleggers used to come into town with their product in gallon jugs, and sell it by pouring it into clear glass bottles from half-pint to quart. Most of their clients were houses of ill repute, and the empties would end up in the garbage cans out back. Which gave Bagoy and the other kids a business opportunity.

"We'd go and reclaim them," Bagoy said, "and put them in a gunny sack and wash them and clean them up and take them downtown and sell them." He can tell you how the federal marshal figured out what they were doing and came to them and said they should report where they found the bottles that smelled like sour mash and each time they did so "I'll give you two bits."

He can tell you how one bootlegger who lived out on the old loop road used to bring his liquor to town in a walled-off part of his gas tank, but he used to give the kids a ride out to Green Lake where they could swim "so we never squealed on him."

He could tell you that and much, much more. But there's more to John Bagoy than talk. For the past 14 years, he's been working to restore the cemetery and put names to some 3,000 unmarked graves. Monday's ceremony is to honor him for that effort. It's to honor the people who put up the money for that effort, too: Ed Rasmuson, CIRI and others. But none of the work would have gotten done without Bagoy, who got started because he saw how rundown the cemetery had become when he went out to tend his father's grave.

"I used to go out and mow the grass, and it was this high," he said, holding his hand three feet off the ground. That's all changed. The city is doing a much better job maintaining the cemetery now, Bagoy said.

Bagoy has done other things to preserve Alaska's history. He's responsible for the founding families exhibit at the museum, and is about to publish a book about pioneer families called "Legends and Legacies." But it's the cemetery, and identifying the graves, that has consumed most of his time and energy.

"It's something I always felt had to be done," he said. "There's a lot of Anchorage out there."

SEPT. 9, 2001

FORTY

NENANA ICE CLASSIC IS ALASKA'S WAY TO PAY COURT TO LADY LUCK

The ice classic is Alaska's longest-running legal gambling enterprise. It was started in 1917, only 50 years after the United States bought the place from Russia.

My father bought ice pool tickets every year. He bought a ticket for every member of the family. After we got to be a certain age, we kids got to pick our own date and time. That continued through high school, college, marriage, our own children. He bought tickets for each of us until 1997, the year he died. I remember thinking that not buying tickets that year meant he was pretty sick.

We never won a dime on the ice pool. As far as I know we were never close. We never won anything on the Irish Sweepstakes tickets he bought every year either. My father was unfazed. Maybe if you were a miner in your youth, as he was, you were a gambler by nature. Maybe that explains why so many men of my father's generation paid court to Lady Luck. Maybe if you lived part of your life thinking the big strike was just over the next hill, the odds against winning the ice pool didn't seem so long.

Maybe that spirit is so embedded in Alaska's culture that laws and sermons can't blast it out. Maybe that's why the bingo halls are full and the rippie joints are flush and you can still find a high-stakes poker game if you know where to look. Maybe that's why the popularity of what we now call the Nenana Ice Classic endures.

The ice classic is Alaska's longest-running legal gambling enterprise. It was started in 1917, only 50 years after the United States bought the place from Russia. To relieve the boredom, Nenana-based workers for the brand-new Alaska Railroad bet on when the ice would go out on the Tanana River. It went out at 11:30 a.m. on April 30 that year. The winner pocketed $800. Good money then, the equivalent of more than $12,000 today.

The ice has gone out on April 30 eight times since, more often than on any other date. The most recent of those April 30ths was the year my father died. The purse that year was $300,000; each of the 14 winning tickets was worth about $21,500. Being the only person to pick closest to the winning day, hour and minute is more lucrative, but harder to do. The last time it happened was 1992, when a welfare mom who lived in Nenana won $165,000.

The ice has always gone out between April 20 and May 20. That should make picking the winning time easier. But there are 44,640 minutes in those 31 days, 44,639 of them wrong. People have concocted elaborate systems to beat those odds, figuring in the temperature, snowfall, the thickness of the ice.

But more often than not the winners used less systematic methods. One of the winners in 1987 said she picked May 5 because five was her lucky number. A 1990 winner combined his street address and apartment number to come up with April 25 at 5:19 p.m. Then there was a winner in 1991 who described his method this way: "I just took a wild guess."

That was always my method, but it didn't work as well for me. Nobody in my family did much better. These dismal results never seemed to discourage my father. He kept buying the tickets, in part because betting on the ice pool is an Alaska thing to do, in part because, as he often told me, "You can't win if you don't play."

He wasn't alone. Last year, people bought 314,000 of the $2 tickets, and when the ice went out May 1 at 10:47 a.m., 18 of them split the $335,000 purse.

Tickets for this year's pool went on sale last week. I didn't buy any tickets last year, or any year since my father died. But I think I will this year. Maybe I'll figure out some way to bet his birthday. That would have made him happy. Besides, you can't win if you don't play.

Feb. 11, 2001

FORTY-ONE

NEW ALASKA CODE DOESN'T SEEM TO INCLUDE STOPPING TO HELP

*But these are not events in Kosovo or New York City or Los Angeles.
These things happened — are happening — right here
on the streets of Anchorage.*

Here are a couple of troubling images from last week's newspaper:

Street people being attacked for sport by teenagers.

A woman, running along a busy street with a bloody baby in her arms, screaming for help and no one stops.

Communication is instantaneous these days. We can, and do, get bad news from around the globe. But these are not events in Kosovo or New York City or Los Angeles. These things happened — are happening — right here on the streets of Anchorage.

I saw one happening the other day myself. I was driving home along Northern Lights Boulevard. It was rush hour. I'd just crossed Denali when I saw a couple of teenagers catch up to a Native man on the sidewalk. One of them threw a punch at the man, who hit back. Then the kid danced around for a minute fake punching like he was some old-timey boxer. By the time I took in what was happening, I was right next to them. I honked. Then I was past. I watched in the rearview mirror as I drove on. Nothing more seemed to be happening. I did not stop. Neither did anyone else.

I did not stop. Want reasons? I've got plenty. I was surprised by what I saw and not ready to react. I couldn't stop, not in bumper-to-bumper traffic that was making a mockery of the speed limit on Northern Lights. I might have been able to pull into one of the driveways along that stretch, and wind back through the parking lots to where the confrontation was happening. It might have been over by then. And if it wasn't, what was I going to do? Tell the kid to quit acting like a punk? Find myself on a busy street arguing with some smart-mouth teenager? Get into a fight and get arrested myself? Sued?

I tell myself that it was no big deal. That if it had been more serious, or if it had been a screaming woman with a bloody baby, I would have stopped. But the fact is, I didn't. And the line between reasons and excuses is sometimes so thin it disappears.

We, the body politic, created much of this teenager-street person problem. We wanted to move street drunks out of downtown so that they wouldn't frighten package tourists from Peoria away from the T-shirt shops. So the city government cut off their downtown supply of cheap, potent alcohol. Then the yups in South Addition made a bunch of noise and closed the next-closest wino-friendly liquor store. Now, the closest supplier is in Midtown. Not every street person wants to make the long, long walk from the homeless shelter every day, so in the summer they move into the greenleaf hotel along Chester Creek.

Don't get me wrong. Street people got preyed on in the old days, too. They are often drunk and make an inviting target. But clumped together, they had mutual support and were easier to police. And punk kids didn't often go down to Fourth Avenue to act out. It was too crowded and public. Now, spread out as they are, the street people are in every way more vulnerable.

I confess, I don't understand why teenagers are assaulting these people. Is it because many of the street people are Native, and, according to the victims, most of the teenagers are white? Or is it simply that street people are easy marks? These kids, with their combination of aggression and cowardice, baffle me.

So do the people who didn't stop for Tammy Grubert as she ran along 15th with a couple of bloody children. What were they thinking? How could they not stop? I'm sure they had their reasons, and I'd like to hear them. I wonder if they'd sound like excuses.

This would not have happened in the Alaska I grew up in. The civic code would not have allowed it. I'd like to act the way I was taught, but the civic code seems different now. How did that happen? How can we change it?

AUGUST 17, 1999

NOME LIKES RICHARD FOSTER MACHINE GUNS, SILENCERS, MORTAR AND ALL

But people in Nome don't scare easy, so it's more likely that a guy with six machine guns is the kind of guy they want representing them in Juneau.

Nome isn't impressed by the indictment of its state representative.

"Nothing's changed since we first heard about it," said Mayor John Handeland. "It's old news here."

Last Tuesday, the federal government hit Richard Foster with a five-count indictment, claiming that he had "six (6) firearms in the form of machine guns fully capable of automatic fire," a couple of silencers, "four (4) machine gun receivers," a sawed-off shotgun and "a destructive device, to wit: a Soviet 50 mm. mortar."

The indictment claims the weapons and weapon parts were unregistered, which makes them illegal. These are big-time charges; each count could be worth 10 years in jail and a $250,000 fine.

Nome, and everybody else, first heard about Foster's problems in March, when federal agents seized some parts Foster had made at a Juneau machine shop, parts they said were for machine guns.

Foster said at the time that he planned to use the parts to build inoperable machine guns for a display at his Nome gun store.

"They were just for a dummy machine gun, like in a movie," Foster said then. "They're making a big deal out of it."

I don't know what Foster's saying now. I left messages all over for him, and one of his aides called back to say Foster's lawyers had asked him not to talk about the indictment. That's too bad. I really wanted to ask him what a guy does with a 50 mm mortar.

Chances are he has a funny answer. This is a man who said of himself, "Everybody thinks I'm going to be an astronaut because I'm taking up space in the legislature."

Foster's not the only one keeping mum. The prosecutor isn't talking much, either.

"The rules of ethics that apply make it inappropriate to comment on the trial evidence," said Assistant U.S. Attorney Mark Rosenbaum.

If I were Rosenbaum, I'd be concerned about my case. Most Alaska towns have more privately owned machine guns than stop lights. So it might be tough to find a jury that doesn't see Foster's case as the failure to fill out some probably unnecessary paperwork. Unless I had solid evidence that Foster was about to invade Chukotsk, or planned to use one of the machine guns to take caribou out of season, I'd be worried about getting a conviction.

Certainly, Foster's colleagues aren't rushing to judgment.

"He hasn't been convicted of anything yet," said House Speaker Sam Cotten. "So I suppose we could try to get all excited about it here, but . . ."

But they all knew about Machine Gun Foster, too. He carried a .50-caliber machine gun through the halls of the state Capitol, joking he was hunting for ultra-liberals. He gave guns as gifts to fellow lawmakers, including Cotten. He is a Vietnam veteran who often wore pieces of his uniform to work and sponsored a resolution supporting former Green Beret Lt. Col. Bo Gritz's wacky plan to reduce Southeast Asian drug traffic.

Like Nome, the legislature took all of this in stride. Having "probably the finest arms collection in the Arctic" was just another quirk there, even when he carried the guns around with him. Having a mortar probably didn't even help Foster get his way in caucuses.

In his hometown, they've rallied round.

Nobody bothered to file against him in the election. That might be because it's not wise to run against a guy with six machine guns. But people in Nome don't scare easy, so it's more likely that a guy with six machine guns is the kind of guy they want representing them in Juneau.

And this fall the residents held a benefit to help Foster pay for his defense, Handeland said.

"Richard never made any secret of the fact he has the guns," Handeland said. "He's a collector of all kinds of items."

Like guns.

And, apparently, friends.

OcT. 2, 1990

NON-THINKERS SPOTTED SATAN AT WORK IN THE HOMER POST OFFICE

Who says pyramids are satanic? I've looked all over the Bible and I can't find where it says that. And if it's not in the Bible, why should anybody believe it?

To tell you the truth, I wasn't at all surprised to read about the outbreak of Satanism in Homer. There are all these artists there, you know, and old hippies and free thinkers. And, if the truth be known, some of those fishermen aren't exactly angels, either. People just don't pay enough attention these days to the threat posed by Satan. His works are everywhere. Movie theaters, art galleries, universities, any place people think. About the only safe places are where people just read the Bible. They don't have to do any of that dangerous thinking, which is just an open invitation to Old Nick to move right in and take over.

Fortunately, at least two people weren't thinking in Homer. One was the person, described only as a pastor's wife, who saw a painting with pyramids in it hanging in the Homer Post Office and complained it was satanic. The other was Homer Postmaster Charlie Arnett, who took the painting, and all others, down faster than you could say "Beelzebub."

Then, so it wouldn't look like Arnett was a spineless weenie, the great big postmaster, Robert J. Opinsky, ordered all art taken off the walls of every post office in Alaska.

And a darned good thing, too. Art does not belong in the post office.

First, it might make you think, and the next thing you know you're out in the woods under a full moon, sacrificing cats to you-know-who.

Second, people might like looking at the pictures. That would be very bad. The post office is a place where you have to stand in line for a long time, bored out of your skull. That's no accident. If it was an interesting place, more people might come. Then half the people who work there couldn't be on break full time.

Third, the pastor's wife might have made good on her threat to tell Sen. Ted Stevens about the pyramids. I'm sure Ted would have raised the devil with the post office, the very thing everybody wanted to avoid in the first place.

So everything turned out for the best. But some questions remain.

Who says pyramids are satanic? I've looked all over the Bible and I can't find where it says that. And if it's not in the Bible, why should anybody believe it?

Why would Satan want to take over the post office? If he's trying to capture souls in Homer, wouldn't he be better off at the health food co-op, where the New Agers hang out? Or maybe someplace where the Lord's name is frequently taken in vain, like the boat launch? What does he get at the post office, besides the headache of trying to get the mail delivered? Even the federal government cut that one loose.

Is the great big postmaster, Robert J. Opinsky, a real person? Nobody I know has ever seen or talked to him. I understand the Postal Service is automating like crazy. Is it possible Alaska already has the first fully automatic postmaster?

And just where will Satan strike next, now that vigilance has been rewarded in Homer? Maybe Juneau, where Walter (6) Joseph (6) Hickel (6) is governor? Or maybe Spenard, although it's pretty clear he's already been there. Will his presence be announced subtly, with pyramids in a painting? Or will it be in the slightly flashier fashion of Revelations: "And behold, a great red dragon having seven heads and ten horns, and on his heads were seven diadems. And his tail swept away a third of the stars of heaven, and threw them to the earth."

If he showed up that way, we wouldn't have to wait for word from the post office to find out about it.

AUG. 2, 1992

NOTHING SAYS "BE MY VALENTINE" BETTER THAN A FLAMETHROWER

*With this much to recommend it, the flamethrower will soon
be as common an accessory on Alaska vehicles as the fuzz
buster and the gun rack.*

The woman who lets me live with her has been out of town. This has had good effects and bad effects at our house. Among the good effects are a huge increase in per capita bacon consumption and a substantial drop in the amount of unnecessary dish washing. Among the bad effects are sharply higher plant mortality and a significant rise in mournful wailing by the cat, particularly during the early morning hours. But the worst effect is that I have been unable to tell her that, this year, her Valentine really, really wants an auto-mounted flamethrower.

The auto-mounted flamethrower was invented by a South African fellow in response to the high number of carjackings in that country. It consists of a canister of liquified gas that flows to nozzles mounted on the car's body. Step on a button near the car's pedals and — whoosh — any bad-nasty standing in front of a nozzle becomes carjacker flambe.

You can see in an instant why this would be a much better Valentine gift than the traditional tokens. Imagine trying to thwart a carjacker by throwing a half-empty box of bon bons at him or smacking him in the mug with a fistful of posies. When it comes to the all-important issue of your loved one's personal auto security, nothing says "Be My Valentine" like a flamethrower.

Now, it's true that carjacking is not a major problem in Anchorage right now, but you never can tell. Alaskans always want to be prepared, particularly when it comes to armaments. But the beauty of the car-mounted flamethrower is that it has a number of other practical applications.

Some examples: The next time the street-cleaning crew blocks your driveway with a mountainous berm, you can simply melt your way to the street. On our many dark winter nights, the flames would help you read street numbers.

And when one of those rolling boomboxes pulls up next to you at a stoplight and threatens to pulverize your liver with its bass, a shot of flame would be just the thing to tell the cretin behind the wheel to turn it down. Not that you'd want to scorch the driver or anything. No. That would be wrong, wrong, wrong. But in addition to convincing him to keep his music to himself, blistered paint might be an effective way of suggesting that he sit up straight, get a haircut and finish his vegetables.

With this much to recommend it, the flamethrower will soon be as common an accessory on Alaska vehicles as the fuzz buster and the gun rack. But it won't work in every dangerous traffic situation. Dealing with a red-light runner, of course, would require fender-mounted surface-to-surface missiles. For moving a pokey motor home out of the way, there's nothing like a 20mm cannon with explosive shells. And you're going to need something that can take out a black helicopter. Face it, each of us should have a vehicle bristling with weaponry. And we have a constitutional right to own one, too.

Unfortunately, unlike so many Alaskans, the woman who lets me live with her is not a constitutional scholar. And she thinks I tend to overreact to traffic problems. So much so, that when she drives us anywhere, her last question before we get into the car is, "Which will it be, the blindfold or the gag?" Besides, she'd probably argue that auto-mounted flamethrowers would simply make driving even more dangerous. But I've got an answer for that one. This is Anchorage, where we have to contend with snowstorms, fog, darkness, icy streets and people zooming down the street with a car phone in one hand and a latte in the other. How much more dangerous could driving be?

FEB. 14, 1999

A REAL ALASKAN'S TIME TO GET READY FOR WINTER IS AFTER IT ARRIVES

"With an attitude like that," he said, "you'll never be a real Alaskan."
And so I learned never do anything until the last minute. Or later.

Wednesday was a great day to be an Alaskan.

An Alaskan who hadn't put on his snow tires yet. Or made sure his snowblower would start. Or even put away his barbecue grill. In other words, a real Alaskan.

I've said it before and I'll say it again, real Alaskans don't get ready for winter. Tell a real Alaskan he'd better get ready for winter, and he'll say, "No way. Winter better get ready for me!"

Of course, real Alaskans who are women are always ready for winter. Or anything else. They have to be, because they have to deal with real Alaskans who are men.

"Isn't it about time to put your snow tires on, Sparky?" the woman who lets me live with her asked last weekend.

"I can't," I said, not taking my eyes off the baseball game on TV, "I have fractured facial bones."

"You use your face to change tires?" she asked.

"Well, sure, whenever the lug wrench slips," I said.

Fortunately, she knew better than to ask me why I didn't take my car to the service station. I'd explained that to her before. A real Alaskan might stop at a service station for gas, if he doesn't have his own tank in the back yard. And he might stop at a service station if he is right in front of one when his entire drive train falls off. But he does all the other vehicle-related chores himself, as long as he has the time, tools and talent. And he does them at the last possible minute.

I learned this from my father, who really was a real Alaskan. He was real Alaskan enough to drive around Fairbanks at 40-below delivering coal while wearing nothing but a light jacket. Even after the driver's-side door fell off. He was real Alaskan enough that all the equipment he owned had seen better days. He was real Alaskan enough to never fix anything until it quit running. And he was real Alaskan enough that when a vehicle did quit running he fixed it himself. (He didn't ever put the driver's-side door back on, he told me once, because "the truck ran just fine without it.")

He used to do the repairs in our front yard. Since the vehicles only broke during the winter, it was always cold. And since he had other work during the day, it was always dark. Which meant he needed someone to hold a light for him.

"Come out from under that bed," he'd bark at me. "I need somebody to hold the light."

Now, it's true you could learn things while holding the light. My older brother learned to fix engines, something he actually likes to do. I learned never to work on vehicles in the cold.

"You know," I told my father once between spells of shivering, "if you'd just fixed this thing when it started to knock, you wouldn't be replacing pistons out here where it's so cold your spit freezes before it hits the ground."

"With an attitude like that," he said, "you'll never be a real Alaskan."

And so I learned never do anything until the last minute. Or later.

That's why, after putting my snow tires on, I was standing in the winter's first real snow Wednesday morning trying to figure out why my snowblower wouldn't start. It had gas. It had oil. Then, as I was feeling around inside to see if the spark plug wire was tight, I tore some skin off a finger. And realized what every real Alaskan knows: No small engine will start until it has had a ritual baptism. With the blood of the guy trying to start it.

Sure enough, it fired on the next pull. Somewhere, I'm sure, my father had a big smile on his face.

Oct. 21, 2001

FORTY-SIX

SADLY, SOME PEOPLE JUST SEEM TO LET THE DARKNESS GET TO THEM

Of course, not every case of depression is a case of SAD. So you might want to get diagnosed before sticking your head in a box of lights.

So we got an hour of daylight back today. Big deal. Darkness is still settling around us like a hand slowly closing into a fist. Like a pillow settling over a face. Like dirt being shoveled into a grave.

Not that it affects me any. Not at all. I'm still the sunny guy I always was. You remember the sun, don't you? Big, bright yellow thing in the sky?

But other people let winter get to them. They get crabby. They sleep more. They eat more junk food. In its severe form, this is a disease called seasonal affective disorder.

"The people I've treated, they define it as there's no meaning to life," said local psychologist Richard Lazur.

I've never been one to take seasonal affective disorder seriously. Maybe it's the dopey name. What's "affective" supposed to mean, anyway? The eggheads probably just strung together some words to make a cool acronym. SAD. Get it? You get SAD, you are sad. This is the kind of cutesy behavior that could really tick me off. If I wasn't always such a happy-go-lucky guy. Not at all the type of person to get SAD.

"Actually, I think a lot of people have mild cases of it and aren't aware they have it," said Lazur. "They'll have an extra candy bar or a cookie, some little comfort food. Then, by mid-December, January, they feel a little more out of it . . . (they) kind of limp along until February or March, by April they're done with it for sure."

OK, so maybe I'm eating a few more candy bars. What's that got to do with anything? I need the calories to cope with the cold.

Actually, SAD has nothing to do with the cold. Or the amount of snow. People begin to suffer this time of the year because daylight is waning. It's the dark that gets you.

The treatment is more light.

"You just stimulate the pineal gland with light," Lazur said. "And it works."

The accepted explanation for the disorder is that, as daylight declines, so does the brain's output of certain chemicals that keep people happy and alert. Sufferers get "sluggish and disinterested and uncomfortable," Lazur said. "Nothing gives them satisfaction."

Daily doses of extra, high-intensity light cause the brain to create more happy-making chemicals, and the sufferer is cured. Lazur recommends "full-spectrum, fluorescent lights that you stare at for an hour in the morning," looking at the light, then away, two or three times a minute. Other experts say any kind of light, if it's bright enough, can work, and the amount of exposure time can vary. Some people use light boxes. Others are experimenting with a gadget that creates a false dawn.

"They now even have little visors, like tennis hats, with the light that shines down in front of you," Lazur said.

Oh, great. Silly hats. All I need is a big bag of chips and a nap, and I'll be fine.

Experts in the field estimate that about 10 million Americans suffer from the full-blown disorder; another 25 million from the milder variety. Naturally, the affliction gets more common as you go north. A study in Fairbanks indicates as many as one in four Alaskans suffers from some form of SAD. All studies say that at least three times as many women as men are sufferers.

Of course, not every case of depression is a case of SAD. So you might want to get diagnosed before sticking your head in a box of lights. Or you could just wait.

"(SAD) is persistent, and typically (people get worse) over time," Lazur said.

Swell. So, say, just for the sake of argument, I have a touch of this disorder, Doc. You sure lights are the best thing for it? Isn't it possible doughnut therapy might work?

"Well, maybe for some people," Lazur said with a laugh. "And, hell, a trip to Hawaii is always good."

Oct. 29, 1995

FORTY-SEVEN

SAVING ANIMALS IS A FULL-TIME JOB REQUIRING HIGH-PROTEIN INTAKE

"Thank heavens that's over," Grandma said. Then she noticed Red Riding Hood looking at her. "Is that meat in that bag, Grandma?" the girl asked. "How could you?"

Little Red Riding Hood was walking through the forest, on her way to Grandma's house with a basket full of macrobiotic goodies, when a wolf came up to her. "Greetings, fellow creature," the wolf said. "Where are you off to?"

"Why, I'm going to Grandma's house," Red Riding Hood said. "She's sick, and I'm bringing her some wonderful spruce bark soup."

"That ought to finish her off," the wolf said to himself. To the girl, he said, "That basket looks heavy. Perhaps I could carry it for you."

"Why, that's extremely non-speciesist of you," Red Riding Hood said. But just as she offered him the basket, an Alaska Department of Fish and Game helicopter full of kill-crazed wildlife biologists flew over. The wolf melted quickly into the brush.

"Murderers," Red Riding Hood shouted, shaking her fist at the helicopter.

The wolf raced through the woods, arriving at Grandma's house well ahead of the girl. He burst through the door and pounced on the bed. No grandma.

"This is a tough place for a guy to get a meal," the wolf said.

After thinking for a while, he donned one of Grandma's green cotton nightdresses, a stocking cap knitted from unbleached yak hair, and a pair of reading glasses. Then he got under the covers and waited. After what seemed like a long time, Red Riding Hood knocked at the door.

"Come in," the wolf said.

Red Riding Hood entered.

"Why Grandma, what a deep voice you have," she said.

"It's this cold," the wolf said. "And do I have a sinus? Whoa boy! But I'm taking wild thyme honey made by free-range bees, and I'm sure my voice will be back to normal soon."

But the girl wasn't really paying attention.

"Why Grandma," she said. "What big teeth you have."

"That tears it," the wolf said. He leaped from the bed and ripped off the nightcap.

"Man, that itches," he said. "I don't know how anybody could get a wink of sleep in one of these things."

"Oh, look," Red Riding Hood said, clapping her hands together. "It's the wolf, pretending to be Grandma. Isn't that darling?"

The wolf stopped dead in his tracks.

"You're a future flight attendant, aren't you kid?" he said. "Here's the situation: I'm a predator. I'm hungry. You're unarmed. Put all that together and what have you got? Lunch."

But as he prepared to leap, the door flew open. In raced a man dressed in camouflage, carrying an M-16 with a banana clip.

"Freeze, hairball," he roared. "I'm game director Dave Kellyhouse, and I have state Board of Game permission to blow you away in order to enhance tourism opportunities."

"Busted," the wolf growled.

Just then Grandma came through the door, carrying a double order of ribs from R.D.'s Bar-B-Q Ranch. She took in the scene and, after setting the ribs down carefully, assumed a karate stance between the wolf and the man.

"Put the gun down, buster," she said. "I'm a charter member of Friends of Animals, and I know Cleveland Amory personally. You harm a hair on his hide and there won't be another tourist in this state before the next ice age. What do you think that'll do to the hotel business?"

"Rats," the man said, lowering his weapon, "a guy can't hardly kill anything anymore."

"You said it," said the wolf, throwing a paw across his shoulder. The two of them left.

"Thank heavens that's over," Grandma said. Then she noticed Red Riding Hood looking at her.

"Is that meat in that bag, Grandma?" the girl asked. "How could you?"

"Why, dear," Grandma said. "I need the protein. Keeping our friends the animals from being slaughtered takes so much energy."

Dec. 27. 1992

SHAKESPEARE WAS WRONG; OUR REAL SALAD DAYS ARRIVE WITH AGE

But the real allure of that time was that we were young and active and could eat impossible amounts of food without gaining weight.

I went out to lunch with a pal of mine the other day, a fellow of maturing years like myself. From a menu chock-a-block with burgers, nachos and other delightful fare, we each ordered a salad. He asked for iced tea. I had decaffienated coffee. When the waiter set our lunches down in front of us, we looked at them, looked at each other and laughed.

Then he told me a story.

When I was young, he said, I got a job as a river rafting guide. They wanted big guys who could carry a lot of heavy stuff, and I was so skinny that I had to lie about my weight to get the job. Part of the pay was that they fed us, so I ate and ate and ate. But I couldn't put on any weight. It got so bad that the guy I worked for paid for me to go to the doctor and get tested to see if I had a tapeworm. He said he'd never seen anybody eat so much without gaining weight.

He shook his head.

Now look at me, he said.

That's what guys our age do now, as we crunch our way through plates of rabbit food. Talk about all the eating we used to do.

Part of the appeal of doing that is we grew up before bacon was declared public enemy No. 1. Back when the only reason you ate oatmeal was that you couldn't afford ham and eggs. Back when, if you were expecting a particularly vigorous day, you'd order your regular breakfast with a steak on the side. Back when eating was eating, not an exercise in nutritional science.

But the real allure of that time was that we were young and active and could eat impossible amounts of food without gaining weight. Now we are no longer very young or very active, and eating a second carrot might mean we won't be able to button our pants.

I don't know why this had to happen. Oh, I'm certain there's a perfectly sound scientific explanation, no doubt involving metabolic and fat absorption rates and lots of other blindingly technical factors. But that's all how it happens. What I want to know is why it happens. What really irritating thing did humans do to God or the gods or nature to make the process of aging such a caloric catastrophe? I guess it's no accident that what Adam and Eve did to get thrown out of the Garden involved eating.

All I know, I told my friend, is that everybody — my doctor, my wife, Richard Simmons — is telling me what to eat and how to eat and, as a result, instead of eating cow, I'm eating like a cow.

Then I told him a story.

I was 17 or 18 and working on a road paving crew out on the Glenn Highway. We all stayed in a roadhouse near Sutton, and room and board was part of the wage. The dining room there was the kind of place where nobody raised an eyebrow if you ordered pork chops and eggs for breakfast. They'd pack us a big lunch and we'd go off to the job for 10 or 12 hours, then come back for dinner. As I recall, every single thing on the dinner menu was fried. The only salad I ever saw was a wilted leaf of lettuce and half a canned cling peach they'd use to decorate the plates if they could keep it out of the gravy.

We'd been there about three weeks or so, long enough to have sampled pretty much everything they had to offer. Then one of the laborers, a guy in his early 20s, noticed that there was some kind of fish on the menu.

Gee, he said, I haven't had the fish yet. I think I'll try the fish.

This was greeted with dead silence. Finally, the head rakeman, a fellow in his 40s, said, I wouldn't be eating that fish if I was you.

Why not? the kid asked.

Well, the rakeman said, fish don't have no blood. And blood, that's where all them vitamins and other stuff are.

Everybody nodded, and the kid ordered the pot roast.

Now, I asked my friend as we got up to leave, why can't I find a guy like that to give me nutritional advice anymore?

Oct. 13, 2000

FORTY-NINE

SHOCKING TABLOID CLAIM: 120-YEAR OLD ESKIMO WOMAN PREDICTS FUTURE

I volunteered to look for Ellekes. It's not every day you get the chance to talk to a 120-year-old person.

Have you heard about Hayda Ellekes?

According to one of the nation's leading tabloids, the *Sun*, Ellekes is a 120-year-old Eskimo woman whose "astoundingly accurate predictions ... are making world experts and psychic investigators gasp in amazement."

Those predictions, the *Sun* reported, have included the start of World War I, the Great Depression and the Good Friday earthquake.

"I have that last prediction on tape," the *Sun* quoted a researcher named Newton Swammerdam as saying.

Ellekes' predictions about the future make her past predictions seem as upbeat as a sunbeam. A huge stock market crash, economic collapse, devastating natural disasters, World War III and the second coming of Jesus Christ will all be squeezed into the next five years. And you thought the '60s were a happening decade.

No wonder the *Sun* put Ellekes on the cover, underneath a teaser for a story about how bananas cure all sorts of ailments.

"Blind great-grandmother is America's Nostradamus," the headline reads, "120-year-old Eskimo woman predicts your future."

The story is given the tabloid's featured position, a full-color, two-page spread. It crowds out even the amazing pizza diet, which not only takes off pounds but cuts the risk of osteoporosis, heart disease and cancer.

One of my colleagues gasped in amazement when he saw all this in the supermarket. Like everyone else I know, he reads tabloids only in the check-out line, but he bought this one and brought it into the office.

"We need to find this woman!" he said. "It says right here that 'she was raised along the Cook Inlet in Alaska, south of Anchorage where she still lives today.'"

I volunteered to look for Ellekes. It's not every day you get the chance to talk to a 120-year-old person. Besides, I thought she might offer some tips on how to get my 401(k) through the coming calamities in the best shape.

But she wasn't in any of the telephone books. Neither was anyone else in the story: her 67-year-old grandson, Geoffrey Torback; Evan Bradman, whose entire family was saved by her earthquake prediction; Swammerdam; the writer of the story, Fred Sleeves.

So I did the one thing I knew would turn up any Alaskan. I looked her up on the list of people who receive the Permanent Fund dividend. She wasn't there. Neither was anybody else mentioned in the story. Including Nostradamus.

"Now that's something that belongs in the tabloids," I told my colleague. "All these people living here and none of them receiving a dividend."

I gave up, called the *Sun* in Boca Raton, Fla., and asked to speak to Sleeves. A woman who said her name is Joan Berkley told me that Sleeves was a free-lancer and that I could fax my questions to her. She'd pass them along, but it was up to Sleeves whether he answered.

I had so many questions for Ellekes, it took me awhile to write them all down: Do you hear voices or see visions? If you could be any animal, what would you be? Would my portfolio benefit from diversification into Portuguese escudos?

When I finished, I couldn't find the fax number. So I went look-ing in the *Sun's* staff box, and found this in teeny, tiny type at the bottom: "SUN stories seek to entertain and are about the fantastic, bizarre and paranormal ... The reader should suspend belief for the sake of enjoyment." My colleague and I concluded that meant the *Sun* might be making it all up.

On the down side, that meant that stories I really wanted to be true — like the one about the pit bull that killed its owners for dressing it like a baby — might not be. On the up side, I could quit looking in vain for an ancient Eskimo prophetess on the Kenai Peninsula. And I was getting tired of eating nothing but bananas and pizza, anyway.

Aug. 22, 1997

FIFTY

THE SMALLEST RITUALS ARE A COMFORT TO THOSE DEALING WITH DEATH

I am not writing this column to thank these people, although I do thank them. I am writing to say each of the messages brought some small solace, and that fact will make me a more certain sender of such messages in the future.

When word of my father's death spread across Fairbanks, food began to arrive.

"Are you still eating ham and potato salad?" I asked my mother a couple of days ago.

"No," she said, "but we still have cookies."

The instinct that led neighbors to feed the huge tribe of Doogans that had assembled must go back to the cave. Its survival in steel-and-glass condo complexes and mud-walled villages around the world is proof of our common heritage. Here and now, it is evidence that in some places beneath the cloud of greed and contention and strife the past 20-odd years have brought to Alaska, community endures.

And it is one more thing. It is a comfort.

The food itself was important. I ate my share. Arriving ready-made, it relieved the tribe's cooks from the labor of feeding the rest of us, at a time when they might have needed their energy for other things. Most important, it was a gesture, a tangible message that in our difficulties we were not alone.

That message helped. At least it helped me. Like many people, I do not look the fact of death in the face until it plants itself unavoidably before my eyes.

We are counseled on the inevitability of death.

"In the midst of life we are in death," the Book of Common Prayer tells us.

"Of all the wonders that I yet have heard,

"It seems to me most strange that men should fear;

"Seeing that death, a necessary end,

"Will come when it will come," Shakespeare wrote.

We know this, but mostly we choose to ignore it. Each death that strikes close to us fills us with wonder, dread, sorrow. We retreat to the cave, to sit around the fire in our skin clothes, pressed close together for the human contact, and perform the rituals of grief and loss, as if for the first time.

And the rituals work.

There was more than food. Flowers arrived at the funeral, as did friends of my father and mother, and of their children and grandchildren. People got up and said kind words. In the weeks since my dad died, I have received cards and calls and messages of sympathy. Some came from close friends. Some from acquaintances. Some from people who, as far as I know, I have never met face to face.

I am not writing this column to thank these people, although I do thank them. I am writing to say each of the messages brought some small solace, and that fact will make me a more certain sender of such messages in the future.

The mother of a childhood friend was in the hospital room next to my father's. The week before, my friend and his family had been certain they were going to lose her. On the telephone, an editor in New York told me of a difficulty she was having over her aging mother in Florida. A card from a woman my age in Kodiak told of the death of her mother. One of my co-workers, also about my age, talked about the death of his father.

We boomers have been marching through life together. Rebellion. Marriage. Career. Parenthood. Arthroscopic surgery. We are now at the place, many of us, when a parent will soon die. When you learn of the death of a mother or father, send a hot dish. Or a card. Or make a call. I'm going to. It is only a small gesture, a minor ritual. But, believe me, it helps.

APRIL 20, 1997

Fifty-One

SOMETIMES IT'S TOO EASY TO FORGET HOW MUCH ALASKA MEANS TO US

I don't blame them. During the two weeks I spent Outside, I didn't see a single vista without buildings or cars or people in it.

I saw Jimmy Barron a couple of weeks ago, lying in a bed in a nursing hospital on a windy hill in San Francisco. He's outlived his knees, but modern medicine is handling that, doctors cutting out the ruined bone and sinew and putting in metal and plastic. Jimmy was recovering from the first surgery, a little fuddled from the drugs and, at 80-plus, frail and arthritic. When you strip off the glitz and smugness of the place that calls itself, simply, The City, peel back the theater openings and patisseries and mink coats for dogs, people like Jimmy are what you find. He was born and raised in San Francisco, went to college there, got married and had a family there, owned property and paid taxes and played golf there. Without middle and working classes full of people like Jimmy, chic and shocking San Francisco would collapse like an empty suit.

Jimmy is a friend of my father-in-law, and in social encounters over the years he and I have built a relationship based on three facts. The college he graduated from was, many years later, the university I graduated from. He's related to a nearly mythical pre-Klondike northern prospector named Leroy Napoleon "Jack" McQuesten. And, while he was in college, Jimmy traveled with a Jesuit missionary named Hubbard on a summerlong trip to the coastal villages of Alaska.

His stories about that trip are full of fun and wonder. When I first heard them, more than 40 years after the fact, they were as vivid as

yesterday. They still are. Maybe he remembers the trip so well because he was young then, but Jimmy surely seems impressed with
what he saw.

Listening to those stories helped me understand why Alaska be-
dazzles so many Americans. Then and now, Alaska is big and empty
and natural in ways the rest of the country isn't. People who visit
leave, like Jimmy, with memories that are small treasures: this mountain, that stretch of empty coast, those bald eagles. But the idea of
Alaska is so powerful that it captures even those who have never
set foot here. "I've always wanted to go there," said a wistful clerk
when she found out where I was from.

Living here, it is easy to forget how powerful the idea of pure
and natural Alaska is. Locked into the groove of daily life, you can
even ignore the streams of tourists who, drawn by that idea, come through
every summer. When we do think of it, we often believe it ourselves;
even in Anchorage we are proud to live so close to nature and survive.
But like everything in life, it has the defects of its virtues. People who
believe in pure and natural Alaska don't want us to build on it and pave it
and drill it. They don't want it to be like everyplace else.

I don't blame them. During the two weeks I spent Outside, I didn't
see a single vista without buildings or cars or people in it. As I was
driving along the freeway after a day of dealing with noise and bad
air and drought and attitude, the idea of Alaska seemed pretty important to me. I thought to myself: If I had to put up with this every
day, I'd send money to the Sierra Club, too. I wouldn't want anybody
drilling that coastal plain, or doing anything else that made Alaska
even a little bit more like this place.

I'm going to remember that the next time I hear some blowhard
say only greenies and lawyers stand between us and the next big
boom. I'll think of Jimmy Barron, too. He's the kind of person we're
going to have to convince that we can drill in the wildlife refuge
without punching holes in his memories. And we're going to have to
prove to frenzied commuters everywhere that we can do it without
wrecking their place of refuge. Even if it's just a place in their minds.

SEPT. 1, 1992

Fifty-Two

TOMATOES NOT ONLY CHEAP CROP THAT COULD BE GROWING IN FAIRBANKS

---

*Perhaps the drug warriors were tipped off by the name of
the place HappyValley Greenhouse or perhaps their sophisticated
electronic eavesdropping devices picked up the
sound of sitar music.*

One of the few good things to come of the U.S. government's war on drugs is cheaper tomatoes in Fairbanks. You might not think that's much return for the billions Uncle Sam has put into a drug enforcement program designed to keep Ronald Reagan and George Bush in office. But this is the federal government we're talking about. Given the way these people normally run their affairs, the citizens of Fairbanks are lucky tomatoes aren't selling for $5,000 a pound.

Uncle Sam got into the tomato business when his drug warriors captured a dangerous greenhouse. In addition to rose bushes and tomato plants, the greenhouse contained that killer weed, marijuana. Smoking marijuana is fun, so it is against the law. I believe the fear is that a nation of stoned Americans would be too happy, hungry and sleepy to keep up the constant vigil against godless communism. Either that, or the liquor lobby greased a few senators.

Perhaps the drug warriors were tipped off by the name of the place Happy Valley Greenhouse or perhaps their sophisticated electronic eavesdropping devices picked up the sound of sitar music. However it happened, they grabbed the place and Uncle got to keep it. Federal law allows the government to seize property without the bother of convicting someone of a crime. Oh, well. Maybe if the government doesn't give due process to suspected drug dealers, there'll be more due process left for the rest of us.

Usually, Uncle sells the property and the drug warriors use the proceeds for cool anti-drug technology. Unless the property is a sports car. Sports cars, it seems, are already cool anti-drug technology.

While the paperwork's being done, federal marshals hang onto the loot. When the loot is a greenhouse, that means keeping the heat on and the plants growing so there will be something besides glass buildings to sell.

So the marshal's office hired a guy with a green thumb to run the operation. He kept producing roses and tomatoes, selling the latter to grocery stores for between $1.65 and $1.85 a pound. And everyone was happy. Right?

Wrong. This is Fairbanks, remember? Where the city motto is, "Oh, yeah? Wanna step outside?"

Sure enough, a rival tomato grower is grousing, claiming that the government-run greenhouse is keeping the price of tomatoes too low. Happy Valley is using public money to subsidize its operation, said Glen Kroshus, and "they are in direct competition with private enterprise."

This is terrible. The next thing you know, the government will be paying farmers not to grow things. Buying crops to keep prices up. Making low-interest loans. Providing cheap land and water. Engineering wheat sales to foreign countries. If this sort of thing isn't nipped in the bud, Uncle will be up to his neck in farming. Then the state will get in. And farming will be nothing more than socialism.

Glen Kroshus is a brave man to take on Uncle Sam. Not to mention saying, in essence, that he wants to stick it to Fairbanks residents with a hankering for fresh tomatoes. I wish him luck.

But what I want to know is this. Why isn't Happy Valley growing marijuana, too?

It'd be a heck of a crime-fighting move. Even with all his spending, Uncle isn't making much of a dent in the drug trade. In Fairbanks, he could just flood the market with subsidized boo and put the local drug lords out of business. Much cheaper. There'd be income, too. Uncle needs every dime to pay off the deficit.

Of course, there might be quicker ways to eliminate the deficit. Maybe the drug warriors could raid the Pentagon, find some seeds and stems, and seize the U.S. armed forces. Who knows? If they can grow cheap tomatoes in Fairbanks, they might be able to buy wrenches for less than $600.

Aug. 3, 1993

Fifty-Three

USUALLY PEOPLE CAUSE THE PROBLEMS, BUT IT'S THE BEARS THAT DIE

The bears would have a point. In most of Alaska, bears spend much
of the year asleep. For the rest, they eat so they can sleep
without starving to death.

If I were writing a column for the bears' newspaper, which I'm sure would be named *The Bear Facts*, here's what I'd say:

"Once again this summer humans are proving what arrogant and bloodthirsty creatures they are. They hunt us. Even when they don't, they come out into our neighborhoods and don't pay attention, and if they run into one of us, they shoot. They live in our territory like we don't exist. They leave their garbage lying around and put plastic lids on their garbage cans and keep rabbits and geese. When one of us shows up to eat, they gawk and take pictures and throw rocks until, one day, one of them pulls out a gun and starts shooting. How fair is that?

"What is the penalty for their ignorant and dangerous behavior? For the humans, it's usually nothing. For us, it's usually death. How fair is that?

"Do you think they'd get away with treating other humans like this? That one of them could fire up the barbecue, throw on some steaks, invite the neighbors over and, when they walk into the yard, shoot them? No way. But when they do essentially the same thing to us, they get off scot-free. How fair is that?"

The bears would have a point. In most of Alaska, bears spend much of the year asleep. For the rest, they eat so they can sleep without starving to death. They are big and quick and lethally equipped, so they have a ferocious reputation. But, really, they do their best to stay away from us.

When man and bear do meet, death is pretty much a one-way street. According to state figures, people killed 59,763 brown and black bears from 1970 through 1996, about 2,300 in self-defense. During the first 85 years of the 20th century, only 20 people died in bear attacks. That's 2,988 bears killed for every person.

The reports we've had this year support these numbers.

In mid-April, hunters killed a brown bear in the backcountry near Paxson in what authorities said looked like self-defense.

In late April, two yearling brown bear cubs were shot and killed in separate incidents near homes in the Haines area.

In mid-May, a man reported shooting and wounding a charging brown bear near Angoon on Admiralty Island.

In early July, a brown bear killed and ate a man who was sleeping under a tarp in a high bear traffic area in Hyder. The bear was killed not long after.

Also in early July, a black bear that was trying to eat some suet balls that a Kenai householder had hung up as bird feeders was shot and killed.

Last week, Fish and Game employees killed three bears around here. One, in Girdwood, had been eating out of garbage bins while tourists watched. The second had been eating pet rabbits on the Hillside. The third had been eating garbage and, maybe, dogs in Eagle River.

Last weekend, a kayaker was bitten in the hip by a brown bear on Admiralty Island.

As long as there are humans and bears, there are going to be unavoidable encounters. Some of them are going to end in death. But many, probably most, of these lethal encounters could be avoided if people behaved themselves. This is particularly true of the encounters in settled areas, where most problems stem from people making bad decisions about what bears think of as food. The most common of those problems is people not keeping their garbage in places where bears can't get at it. But they also put out food for birds like they're living in some California suburb and keep other pets and pet food in places where bears can get at them. This is inevitably bad news for the bears.

"If people don't keep these bears from getting into the bird feed and the garbage, then the bears are going to learn bad things and have to be destroyed," said Fish and Game's Rick Sinnott.

Sinnott is right. Bears are smart. They learn things. Too bad people don't.

JULY 28, 2000

"VICTIM 5: 'I WANT THAT FELONY ASSAULT TO STICK TO HIS RECORD'"

She has been told that in the plea bargain being negotiated between the prosecutor and Poindexter's lawyer, the assault charge will be dropped. She doesn't like the sound of that either.

She has a picture of herself from before the attack. She carries it in a folder with newspaper clippings and her medical report. In the picture, she's sitting with a friend and they're both laughing and you can see the laugh lines in her left check and around her left eye.

If she were to laugh today, those lines wouldn't show. Not since they put the plate in her face.

"This man did a lot of damage to me," she said.

This man, police say, is Gregory Lemon Poindexter. Poindexter is accused of kidnapping and raping five Alaska Native women between August of last year and January of this year. She is the last victim, Victim 5. He has been charged with 14 counts of sexual assault, three counts of kidnapping and one count of assault. The assault charge comes from what happened to Victim 5.

The physical damage is listed in her medical report: left orbital floor fracture, nasal fracture, lacerations of the upper and lower lips, gingival lacerations, hypesthesia of intra-orbital nerve, left side, three fractured teeth, chemosis, conjunctival hemorrhage, diplopia, contusion of eyelid, multiple contusions, mild hypothermia.

She pointed farther down on the page.

"A lot of this neck and back pain is from him grabbing my hair and jerking me around," she said. "I had a big ball of hair taken out of my head."

The metal plate is where the left orbital floor, the bone that runs under her left eye, used to be. The lacerations of the upper and lower lips required 24 stitches to close. The diplopia is double vision in her left eye, which accounts, at least in part, for the sunglasses she wears now. She doesn't know what chemosis is.

"But I don't like the sound of it," she said.

She has been told that in the plea bargain being negotiated between the prosecutor and Poindexter's lawyer, the assault charge will be dropped. She doesn't like the sound of that either.

"That's very upsetting because I've had to live with this," she said. "I still have to look at this in the mirror. . . . I have people who still don't recognize me. . . . I want that felony assault to stick to his record."

She was kidnapped about 3 a.m. on Jan. 25 near 13th and Gambell.

"I think I was grabbed because I was vulnerable," she said. "Yes, I was intoxicated."

She was taken to the upper Hillside, where, over the next two hours, she was assaulted. The police found her blood and the frames of her eyeglasses in Poindexter's truck, she said. They have other evidence as well. But the thing is, she can't identify him.

"In that vehicle, he was in my face. . . . I was so terrified. I could see his face clearly then, but I can't now. . . . I don't understand why. . . . I don't understand how I cannot identify him today. I was with him for two and a half hours."

Maybe it was what happened to her. During the hour or so we talked, she circled back through that part of her story, sometimes agitated, sometimes matter-of-fact. Here's some of it.

"I could tell the hit was coming. I said, 'Please don't hit me. What did I ever do to you?' I blocked it, like this." She crossed her wrists in front of her face. "I felt the first hit but not the second or the third. . . . I went down on my knees. . . . He kept hitting me . . . He stopped and said, 'I'm going to teach you Native bitches a lesson,' . . . and it gets more graphic."

She is a local woman, 36, small, well-spoken, a graduate of East High with three semesters at Sheldon Jackson that were ended, she said, by alcohol.

Before the attack, she said, "I was on the road of life." She had a new job working on the North Slope until this spring and figured she'd earn enough money "either for a new vehicle or the down payment on a new home." She was looking forward to having this summer off because "I love to go camping and fishing."

Since the attack, she has been keeping doctor's appointments and trying to deal with the emotional damage.

"As I'm telling my story, each time, I'm trembling, I get upset," she said. "I've encountered almost every emotion a person can feel."

She is suspicious of strangers now. She is afraid to walk her dog at night. She hasn't been able to go near the area where she was assaulted.

"I used to love to take a drive up to Flattop," she said. "I loved the view up there. It's too much of a heavy reminder, negatively. There's been days I do want to go up. I've thought about it a hundred times. I want my courage back."

Good things have happened, too, though, she said. "I didn't realize the friends I had in my life until they came forward after they heard what happened to me." And if the plea bargain should go forward, "I have no choice but to accept it. That's the best way to handle this. If I don't, it will slow down my healing process."

"I'm working on my forgiving," she said. "I've always been taught to forgive."

AUG. 28, 2001

FIFTY-FIVE

WEALTH OF SHOW BIZ EXPERIENCE HELPS HARPER COPE WITH ADVERSITY

"The career that followed included a little bit of everything: serious drama, voice work, improvisation, live television, whatever would pay the rent in San Francisco, Los Angeles and Seattle."

Jerry Harper took the news that he'd have to cancel the remaining performances of his spectacular production of *The Metamorphosis* without flinching. One of the actors needed surgery, and there was no understudy. End of run. His Eccentric Theater Company really could have used the money from four more performances in the pocket-sized, 88-seat theater adjoining Cyrano's Bookstore and Cafe. But 50 years in show business have given him oodles of perspective. He sat for a moment, preoccupied.

"I'm just trying to figure out, what do we fill with?" he said.

The question reflects the state of theater in Anchorage. During the oil boom, the Alaska Repertory Theatre was known throughout the country as a place where visiting actors got the best treatment money could buy. But as the oil money dried up, the Rep went out of business. The small companies that remain lead a hand-to-mouth existence.

They are almost back to the level of theater Harper remembers from the mid-1940s. His parents brought him, a 14-year-old, north in 1944, when Anchorage was a town of 11,000. His first stage experience was with the Anchorage Community Theater, including a production of *The Warrior's Husband,* which he recalled "had a lot of young girls in it." He played Ajax.

"I had about two lines," he said. "I remember them well. 'Achilles? Is he here?' "

Harper has been acting ever since. He earned a theater degree at an Oregon college, then did graduate work at Washington State. Summers, he did summer stock.

"I guess my first paying job was at the Old Brewery Playhouse in Helena, Montana," he said. "We did *The Fourposter*, *Abie's Irish Rose*, all those old war horses. But it was wonderful experience."

The career that followed included a little bit of everything: serious drama, voice work, improvisation, live television, whatever would pay the rent in San Francisco, Los Angeles and Seattle.

"An actor who isn't really well known, who can't pick and choose, is after anything he can get," Harper said.

The same oil bust that killed the Rep brought Harper back to Anchorage, and he brought his wife, Sandy, a fellow actor he'd met in 1962. Harper had inherited the building on D Street from his mother. It's an old building — the theater dates from the 19-teens — and the Harpers borrowed money to fix it up. That was finished just as the mid-'80s bust hit.

"So we came up as a matter of desperation, to save the building," he said.

Today, Sandy and Jerry — most everyone who knows them refers to them as a unit — operate the bookstore, cafe and theater, enduring financial ups and downs. Jerry's acting here — he has played everything from Shylock in *The Merchant of Venice* to Teach in *American Buffalo* — has been interrupted by surgery to remove a brain tumor and limited by the "physical impairments that come with age." At 66, with close-cropped black hair and a trim, white beard, Jerry no longer considers himself for many lead roles. But he did play the senior Samsa in *The Metamorphosis*, as well as producing and directing. Next, he said, he'll play Polonius in *Hamlet*.

Those, and all the other roles he's had, the plays he's been able to produce and direct, seem to Harper to be adequate compensation for being up here out of the mainstream, struggling.

"I never regretted a minute of it," Harper said. "It's the work that counts."

DEC. 6, 1998

FIFTY-SIX

WHEN A DAUGHTER GOES OFF TO COLLEGE, A FATHER BEGINS TO FEEL OLD

Despite all the changes, I'm sure my daughter will find the bay area an exciting place to attend college. Heck, maybe she'll even go to some classes, something I know I always meant to do.

My daughter leaves for college tomorrow. My youngest child. The next day, I'm going to pick out my room at the Pioneer Home. Not really. Look at my photo. Doesn't that look like a man who's got a couple of years of independent living left? Just don't sass me, or I'll whomp you with my walker.

The child is going to Berkeley. No, it's OK. I checked. Mario Savio is not the dean of students there, and most people are clothed most of the time. True, there is a small band of naked persons that shows up from time to time. But I understand the riot squad has quit busting heads and the wind has blown most of the tear gas out to sea. So I figure, what's a naked person more or less?

Besides, this young lady is much better prepared than I was for the oddities of American civilization. She's made several trips Outside, so she knows where to find The Gap and how to use Mace. When I went to college, it was the first time I'd ever been to America.

By the way, did I tell you that when I was a child, we lived in a hole in the road? And were darn grateful to have it, too.

Nearly 30 years ago it was, I boarded a Boeing 707 belonging to an airline long since bankrupt and flew to the same airport my daughter's headed toward. No, I wasn't going to Berkeley. No way. Instead, I was enrolled in a small Catholic college across the bay in

San Francisco. My father figured the Jesuits would take care of me. He was right; I haven't been to church since.

I was how should I put this? a rube. For several years I thought San Francisco was overrun with cultural facilities, because the cabbie who drove me in from the airport passed the opera house three times.

"Yep," he said, "we love our culture here in The City. That'll be $57."

Many things have changed since then. For one thing, I understand that you can only communicate with the cab drivers in Hindi. For another, according to the stuff my daughter has been getting in the mail, college students can now have certain types of cooking equipment in their dorm rooms.

This was absolutely forbidden in my day. If we'd been able to cook in our rooms, the cafeteria would have been as empty as the chapel. I've forgotten a few things about college, but the food, unfortunately, isn't one of them. Who could forget Mystery Meat? Jell-O so rubbery you could dribble it? And the mashed potatoes you had to eat quick because, once they set up, you couldn't have chipped a mouthful off with a jackhammer?

No in-room cooking also meant that whenever we got hungry late at night, we had to sneak down to the corner grocery. It was run by a couple of Lebanese guys, which is why, to this day, I can say "potato chips" in Arabic. Those of you who went to college before Nancy Reagan became president might remember why we needed potato chips late at night. Or, come to think of it, maybe not.

Despite all the changes, I'm sure my daughter will find the bay area an exciting place to attend college. Heck, maybe she'll even go to some classes, something I know I always meant to do. She is, after all, not just more sophisticated than I was as a college freshman, she's more mature, too. Not just more mature than I was then; more mature than I am now.

Instead of hanging around places like the Fillmore Auditorium and Winterland like her old man, she'll no doubt be going to museums and galleries and theaters. Who knows, perhaps she'll actually see the inside of the opera house. Then she can drop by during spring break and shout a description of it into my ear trumpet.

Aug. 9, 1994

FIFTY-SEVEN

WHOA, DUDE, ON TELEVISION THIS ALASKA PLACE IS, LIKE, TOTALLY FUNNY

If you don't like these plots, make up your own. Start by watching the premiere this spring to see for yourself.

I just finished watching the pilot for the new Fox sitcom set in Anchorage.

It's about these three late 20s, early 30s guys who live in a big house that sits all by itself on a beautiful lake, just like the houses we all live in. Billy, who looks like Michael J. Fox, only taller, is an architect. Reed, who looks like Clint Walker, only cuter, owns an outdoor adventure company. Andy, who looks like the guy who used to play Mac on *Magnum*, only dweebier, is an Air Force security officer. They spend their time fishing for 10-foot trout and drinking beer and being horny.

So it's pretty realistic.

Anyway, Reed's brother Matt, who looks like one of those guys on the commercial who are always doing a Dew, only dumber, used to be their roommate, but he got married. So they need a new roommate.

Who should show up but Kate, who looks like Suzanne Somers, only younger. Kate has just arrived to work for a resort company and needs a place to live. After a lot of jokes about sex and dead animals that really cracked up the laugh track, she decides to move in. Then she breaks up with her boyfriend in LA, so the guys take her to the brewpub Matt owns, where the patrons are wearing more flannel than I've seen since the last Eddie Bauer catalog. More sex jokes have the laugh track in stitches. She gets hammered, and puts the moves on Reed, then Billy. By now, the laugh track is rolling on the floor. But before anything can happen, Kate passes out and the guys just can't take advantage of her. As the pilot closes, they're all friends.

By then I'm thinking, major hit. I can hardly wait for the one where Billy's mom shows up and Kate has to pretend she's gay so mom won't think there's any funny business going on.

But you know how it is with some TV series. They start out boffo, and just can't maintain the same level of wit and sophistication. Besides, the guy in charge of the show has only been to Anchorage three times, so he might have trouble coming up with more of these realistic plot lines.

Fortunately, I have a few ideas. Real Anchorage ideas.

How about one where they all go back to the brewpub and Kate gets hammered again, only instead of that making her even cuter she ends up wrapped around a toilet. And everybody else in the place gets blotto, too, and there's a big fight in the parking lot.

Or, the day of the first snow Kate slides through an intersection and T-bones an unemployed welder who hires a lawyer he picked out of a TV ad and sues her for her back teeth.

Or, as winter progresses, the cold and dark make Kate so depressed she starts bingeing and gains 40 pounds. Sally Struthers could play the fat Kate.

Or, because Reed's hunting and fishing rights have been violated by the federal government, he joins a ring that smuggles illegally killed animal trophies Outside.

Or, Billy is indicted for bribing a public official to give a contract to his architectural firm, but plea bargains his way out of jail time.

Or, Andy is abducted by aliens, but the other Air Force security officers tell Kate the alien spaceship was really swamp gas.

If you don't like these plots, make up your own. Start by watching the premiere this spring to see for yourself. The show is on Fox, which is kind of like a television network, only hipper. It's called *The Last Frontier*.

And people say there's nothing good on TV.

JAN. 28, 1996

FIFTY-EIGHT

WITH THE HELP OF DATABASE AND $16 DRESS, WEDDING IS A SUCCESS

So, you're saying to yourself, this schmo thinks the whole wedding was totally about him. But that's not true. It was just mostly about me.

"Well," I said to the woman who lets me live with her as we stood in the receiving line, "we did it."

And, in fact, we did. Well, actually she did it and I watched. But why split hairs? Our daughter was successfully married, feted and sent off. All that's left is the cleanup. My part of that is applying to the International Monetary Fund for an emergency loan to stave off bankruptcy. I figure that since they give billions to everybody from Argentina to Zimbabwe, they can front me enough to pay for this wedding.

Cost aside, the wedding was a complete success from my point of view. I managed to maneuver the bride down the aisle without injuring anyone, say my one line without flubbing, read a selection from Edgar Allan Poe without giving in to a powerful urge to cackle ghoulishly, and look damn good in a tuxedo while doing all that.

So, you're saying to yourself, this schmo thinks the whole wedding was totally about him. But that's not true. It was just mostly about me. The parts that weren't about me, as insignificant as they might have been, went fine, too.

Like the mother of the bride's dress. After buying and returning more than $1,000 worth of frocks, the woman who lets me live with her settled on a dress that, because it was on sale and she had a coupon, cost her $16. (That's not counting, of course, the cost of the jacket and a pair of shoes she'll never wear again.) Still, many more people complimented her on her dress than complimented me on my tuxedo. Go figure.

What really seemed to go well, though, was the gift getting. Now, I'm sure the etiquette fuddy-duddies frown on talking about the gift-getting aspects of weddings. But I mean, really. Our daughter was opening wedding gifts from the moment she hit dirt here until the moment she departed. Appliances. Dishes. Do-re-mi. You name it, the newlyweds got it.

About the fourth or fifth day of frantic unwrapping, I leaned over to the woman who lets me live with her and whispered, "Look at this loot. Maybe we should renew our vows."

"That would violate one of my basic rules of life," she replied.

"What's that?" I asked.

"Never make the same mistake twice," she said.

She obviously was well aware of the wedding's gift-getting potential, because she'd designed a gift section right into her wedding database.

That's right. Not content with creating or organizing every aspect of the wedding, the woman who lets me live with her designed a computer database to keep track of it all. The database contained the name and address of everyone who had been invited, who had put them on the invitation list, whether they responded, how many people were coming, what their blood types were and who they had voted for in the three previous presidential elections. Plus what gift they'd given. So while the bride-to-be was clawing wedding paper off of boxes, her mother was filling in the gift section in the database. For the thank-you cards.

Thank-you cards are the bride's share of the cleaning up. Thanking the right people for the right gift is, it turns out, essential. So essential that one of the bride's uncles was dispatched to the reception with a roll of tape in his pocket, so that he could tape each card firmly to each gift.

That, plus the database, means the bride can write her thank-you cards swiftly and surely. And we can all move on to other things. Like figuring out how to pay for all this if the IMF doesn't come through.

JUNE 12, 2001

WOMAN GETS $2,600 WORTH OF GOOD NEWS FROM THE POST OFFICE

How did the prospect of losing $2,600 feel? "It's only money," she said.
"It's not the end of a friendship, it's not the end of the world,
it's only money."

Colleen White figured out what happened to the money about 3:30 a.m.

"From 11:30 until 3:30 in the morning, I'm thinking somebody stole it," she said. "Then I realize my error, exactly what I'd done."

White had put $2,600 in cash in an unsealed, unmarked envelope that ended up in the mail.

Here's how that happened.

White has had her own business for more than 10 years, making scarves and sweaters and Christmas tree ornaments from the soft, dense undercoat of the musk ox, called qiviut. The items aren't cheap.

"A sweater can cost $1,400," White said.

Once in a while someone pays with greenbacks. White usually whisks the money right to the bank. But she had been letting it accumulate to open an account for building a winter home in Mexico. In the envelope were 25 $100 bills, two $50 bills, some notes about the house to be and a pinch of dirt.

"The dirt was from a shrine in New Mexico," she said. "I was blessing the money because this was the beginning of our money to build our retirement home."

On June 15, a Monday, White was at home in Palmer, preparing to go to her Sheep Mountain studio for the week. The envelope was on the stairs with some letters to be mailed. Her plan was to make a run to the bank and post office before she left. Instead, her assistant, Mollie Boyer, asked if she could help by taking the mail to the post office.

"After raising seven children," White said, "my usual response to any question like that is, 'Yes.'"

Boyer scooped up all the envelopes, took them to the Palmer post office, and dropped them into the box. White went to Sheep Mountain and didn't give the money another thought until she got back to Palmer at the end of the week. In the wee hours, she figured out what had happened.

"At 5:30, I tell Mollie that not only am I part of this, she is too," White said. "So she can't sleep."

White called the post office, and was told she'd have to send a letter to the mail recovery center in San Francisco. That did not strike her as a good sign.

"I knew I was going to go through the steps to pursue it," she said, "but I didn't have any idea I'd see it again."

How did the prospect of losing $2,600 feel?

"It's only money," she said. "It's not the end of a friendship, it's not the end of the world, it's only money."

White sent the letter June 22, a Monday morning.

"Then I tell Fred at the Palmer post office," White said, "and everybody's abuzz."

The mail gets some sorting in Palmer, but most of the work is done at the Anchorage airport facility. Boyer drove into Anchorage to check, and the Palmer superintendent called Anchorage. Eventually, White was told to call Robert Fineman at the Anchorage post office.

Fineman supervises a sorting crew there. They were doing their usual job, when somebody noticed $100 bills rolling along a conveyor belt. They backtracked the bills to the envelope, saw there was no way to tell whose money it was, and passed it along to Willie Kinnebrew in customer services.

"We counted it," Kinnebrew said. "We put it into an account, which is a trust account to see if anybody claimed it."

When White called, they asked her to identify the money. She told them how much there was, and told them about the note. Satisfied, they made out some money orders and sent them to White in Palmer.

"It's very rewarding to be able to make a happy customer," Kinnebrew said.

White was so happy that she's sending a donation to Fineman's favorite charity, Big Brothers and Big Sisters. And telling everybody what happened.

"These people were marvelous," White said. "All those terrible things you hear about the postal service, I use them so much, to send things all over the world and get things from all over the world. They've been nothing but absolutely great with me."

June 5, 1998

YOU HAVE TO GROW OLD, BUT HERE'S PROOF YOU DON'T HAVE TO GROW UP

We've been friends for 40 years.We have jobs and mortgages and grown kids of our own. But when we get together, none of that matters.

My best friend turns 46 today. He's getting old. He has Alfred Hitchcock's silhouette now. And Walter Brennan's walk. If hair was money, his head would be an S&L. We've been friends since we were kids. Kindergarten, or maybe first grade. I'm not sure which. When I think back, I can't remember a time when we weren't friends. Except when one of us got mad and we went to Fist City. If hot temper was potatoes, he'd be Ireland. The Republic and the five counties both.

In fact, he's as Irish as peat fires. As rain. As car bombs. Irish on both sides of his family. So he's got the gift of gab.

"That child didn't just kiss the Blarney Stone," my Irish grand-mother said long ago, "he swallowed it."

My pal never let this talent get rusty from lack of use. If a win-dow got broken, he'd tell the offended homeowner that he'd only just borrowed my baseball bat to keep a rabid dog from biting an orphan. Honest. He didn't play baseball himself, he'd explain. Weak heart.

The guy's no different today. If blarney was bologna, he'd be Oscar Mayer.

When he wasn't getting us into hot water, he had two broth-ers, not much younger than he was, who were. They lived a few blocks down the street. Not far. But then, in Fairbanks in the 1950s, nothing was far. The four of us developed an unfortunate and undeserved reputation in our neighborhood. When they saw us coming, mothers snatched small children off the street. Vegetable gardeners ran for their shotguns. Mean dogs whimpered.

Summers we had pretty much to ourselves. We had chores, but otherwise we went where we wanted and did what we wanted and took the beatings when we got caught. Winters we went to the Catholic school and caused nuns to have doubts. Then, in the fifth or sixth grade, his family moved to Anchorage.

Losing your best friend is fairly high up on the list of childhood traumas. But when my family followed five or six years later, he and I picked right up where we left off. Friendship, it turned out, is portable. It can stay with you not just through space, but through time.

As teen-agers, we hung around the pool hall and played poker with a bunch of guys of such questionable morals many of them grew up to be lawyers. We drove up Fourth Avenue and down Fifth that was "cruising the gut" in a much smaller Anchorage and tried to get our hands on beer. In the summers, we worked. Winters we went to school and caused teachers to change careers. We watched fights and, every once in a while, got into one. We were jerks to girls. What can I say? We were teen-aged boys, it was in the job description then. If class was water, we'd have been the Sahara desert.

Except for getting older and slightly taller, my pal didn't change much. You should have heard him explaining to the Anchorage cop why we were driving out of the Family Market parking lot with a crate of eggs in the car.

After high school, he went his way and I went mine. Since then, we've sometimes lived in the same town, sometimes not. I've laughed a lot more the times we have. Right now, he lives down the street, just like when we were kids. We don't make mean dogs whimper anymore, but we can buy our own beer.

When we're having lunch today, I won't say anything profound about our friendship. Instead, I'll tell him how very, very old he looks. He'll remind me that I'm a week older than he is. Might call me a name or two as he does it. Then I'll say something back, and we'll carry on like a couple of kids.

We've been friends for 40 years. We have jobs and mortgages and grown kids of our own. But when we get together, none of that matters. If maturity was dry land, we'd be Potter Marsh.

JUNE 14, 1994

ABOUT THE AUTHOR

Mike Doogan was born and raised in Alaska, the son of pioneer Alaskans Jim and Jerry Doogan. He is 54. He graduated from West Anchorage High School in 1966, received a BA in English from the University of San Francisco in 1970 and an MFA in Creative Writing and Literary Arts from the University of Alaska Anchorage in 1999.

Doogan has been a journalist and writer throughout his adult life. He worked for the now-defunct *Anchorage Times*, beginning as a sports reporter and ending as editor of the Sunday paper. Following a foray into state politics as a campaign manager, legislative aide and consultant, he joined the *Anchorage Daily News* as an editor in 1985. For the past thirteen years, he has written a three-days-a-week Metro column. His columns have been collected in <u>The Best of the Rest</u> and <u>Society: An Alaskan Perspective</u>. His writing has received awards from the National Education Writers Association, the Society of Professional Journalists, the Best of the West competition and the Alaska Press Club.

Doogan is the author of numerous magazine articles and two books of nonsense about Alaska, *How to Speak Alaskan* and *Fashion Means Your Fur Hat Is Dead*. He is the editor of and a contributor to a book of essays by longtime Alaskans, *Our Alaska*.

Doogan is married. He and his wife of thirty-three years, the long-suffering Kathy, have two children; Matt, 29, and Amy, 26.

RECOMMENDATIONS FOR READERS INTERESTED IN KNOWING MORE ABOUT ALASKANS AND HOW THEY LIVE

AMAZING PIPELINE STORIES
How Building the Trans-Alaska Pipeline
Transformed Life in America's Last Frontier
by Dermot Cole, paperback, $14.95

COLD RIVER SPIRITS
The Legacy of an Athabascan-Irish family
from Alaska's Yukon River
by Jan Harper-Haines, hardbound, $19.95

FASHION MEANS YOUR FUR HAT IS DEAD
A Guide to Good Manners and Social Survival in Alaska
by Mike Doogan, paperback, $14.95

IDITAROD DREAMS
A Year in the Life of Sled Dog Racer DeeDee Jonrowe
by Lew Freedman, paperback, $14.95

OUR ALASKA
Personal Stories about Life in the North
edited by Mike Doogan, paperback, $16.95

RAISING OURSELVES
A Gwitch'in Coming of Age Story from the Yukon River
by Velma Wallis, hardbound $19.95,
softbound $14.95